DEFENDING
MY
ENEMY

OTHER BOOKS BY ARYEH NEIER

CRIME AND PUNISHMENT: A Radical Solution
DOSSIER: The Secret Files They Keep on You

DEFENDING MY ENEMY

American Nazis, the Skokie Case, and the
Risks of Freedom

ARYEH NEIER

E.P. Dutton · New York

For information contact:
E.P. Dutton, 2 Park Avenue,
New York, N.Y. 10016

Library of Congress Cataloging in Publication Data

Neier, Aryeh, 1937-
Defending my enemy.
Includes index.
1. Liberty of speech—United States. 2. Assembly,
Right of—United States. 3. National Socialist Party
of America. 4. American Civil Liberties Union.
5. Skokie, Ill.—Demonstration, 1977. 6. Jews in the
United States—Politics and government. I. Title.
KF4772.N43   323.4′0973   78-10180

ISBN: 0-525-08972-1

Published simultaneously in Canada by
Clarke, Irwin & Company Limited, Toronto and Vancouver

Designed by Nicola Mazzella

10 9 8 7 6 5 4 3 2 1

First Edition

**FOR
WOLF NEIER
1899-1966**

Contents

Prologue

"My only hope," said a letter I received from a man in Boston, "is that if we are both forced into a march some day to some crematorium, *you* will be at the head of the parade, at which time you will in your rapture have an opportunity to sing hosannas in praise of freedom of speech for your tormentors."

I have received many similar letters. They were provoked by the efforts of the American Civil Liberties Union, which I served as executive director, to secure free speech for a group of American Nazis who said they wanted to march in Skokie, Illinois. The most succinct letter was from the man who proposed a motto for the ACLU: "The First Amendment *über Alles.*"

While it was painful to receive those letters, one woman's message of support was more disturbing. "I love free speech," she wrote, "more than I detest the Nazis." Like the people who denounced me, she thought a choice had to be made between upholding free speech and fighting the Nazis. She just made a different choice.

I made no such choice. I supported free speech for

1

Nazis when they wanted to march in Skokie in order to defeat Nazis. Defending my enemy is the only way to protect a free society against the enemies of freedom. If that seems to be a paradox, I hope it will not be when you finish reading this book.

My reasons for hating Nazis are personal as well as philosophical. I could have written back to the man who expressed his hope that I would head the parade to the crematorium, saying that I narrowly missed dying there.

I am a Jew, born in Berlin. My parents were *Ostjuden* (Jews from Eastern Europe) who left their families in Poland and went to Berlin in the years after World War I. The 1920s were good years for them. They built comfortable lives. But by the time I was born, in 1937, the world of my parents was crumbling. Although many of his friends had already left, my father, Wolf Neier, who was then employed by the Berlin Jewish Community as a teacher of Hebrew, stayed on in Berlin. We did leave, finally, in 1939, at what was probably for us the last possible moment. We escaped to England. My ten-year-old sister, Esther, went by herself. My father traveled separately from my mother and me. I got out of Germany in August 1939, days before the outbreak of World War II in Europe.

We were not reunited immediately. The British took time to separate refugees from spies and saboteurs. After my father survived that sifting process, he had to find a job and earn some money to reassemble the family. I spent a year in a hostel for refugee children. It is an experience I recall vividly. The hostel was a miserable place. I hated it.

Not long after the family was reunited in London, our house was destroyed in a bombing attack. We were evacuated to a Midlands town and, after a period of boarding in the home of a gracious and generous English family, found a place of our own to live.

When the war ended, my parents discovered what had happened to their families. Almost everyone was dead. Only fragmentary information was available on how they had been murdered. My father's mother had been shot and killed early in the war, soon after the Germans overran the village in Poland where she lived. Two of my mother's brothers had survived in Bergen-Belsen until the end, only to be killed on the eve of the camp's liberation. Others died along the way.

In Northampton, England, where I spent the years immediately after the war, a friend of my parents established a group home for Jewish boys who had survived the death camps. My father and my sister became their teachers. I spent much of my time with them and they became my friends. They were the first death-camp survivors I met. I learned a little about how they escaped the crematoria. Yosie, who was only fourteen when he came to England and looked much younger, had lived in the woods for four years, much of that time entirely by himself. Janek lived because he entertained the camp guards with his singing and accordion playing. Another survived—I now deduce from his appearance and by recalling what the others said at the time —because the guards found him so beautiful.

I recite my own background to suggest why I am unwilling to put anything, even love of free speech, ahead of detestation of the Nazis. Many residents of Skokie, Illinois, have far better grounds for detesting the Nazis. They themselves experienced the death camps. I know those horrors only through the words of others. They watched the Nazis kill members of their families. I was too young ever to know the members of my family who died in the camps and I was hundreds of miles away in England when they died. I could not bring myself to advocate freedom of speech in Skokie if I did not believe that the chances are best for preventing a repetition of the Holocaust in a society where every incursion on freedom is resisted. Freedom has its risks. Suppression of freedom, I believe, is a sure prescription for disaster.

In describing my childhood brushes with Nazi terror, I do not hope to mitigate the anger of the man who wants to see me lead the parade to the crematorium. It would do no good. Most Jews know other Jews who are so filled with self-hatred that they are the worst anti-Semites. I have been put in that category, I suppose, by many of the letter writers who denounce me so bitterly for defending free speech for Nazis.

The most frequently repeated line of all in the many letters about Skokie that I received was: "How can you, a Jew, defend freedom for Nazis?"

In thinking about the answer to that question during the many months when the letters poured in, I found my own sense of Jewishness deepening. The response I made, perhaps illustrating a trait reputed to be characteristic of Jews, most often began with a question: "How can I, a Jew, refuse to defend freedom, even for Nazis?"

Freedom is no certain protection. The risks are clear. If the Nazis are free to speak, they may win converts. It is possible that they will win so many adherents that they will attain the power to abolish freedom and to destroy me.

John Milton's view that truth will prevail in a free and open encounter with falsehood is my view, too. I want to keep encounters between ideas free and open, expecting to give truth the edge. But I cannot accept Milton's principle as infallible. In this century that has seen so much evil, I must be wary of putting too much faith in any principle of human behavior. And I must examine with care the alternatives that are available to me. My freedom—and my life— may depend on the choice.

The alternative to freedom is power. If I could be certain that I could wipe out Nazism *and* all comparable threats to my safety by the exercise of power, perhaps I would be tempted to choose that course. But we Jews have little power. We are few in number. We are known by the world as a separate race and a separate religion. Only Jews are doubly marked as a people apart.

The rest of the world is suspicious of us Jews. We are

like each other and we will stick by each other, the world believes. If a scapegoat is needed for any evil, look among Jews and accuse all Jews. If a Jew took part in the Crucifixion, all Jews are Christ killers. If a Captain Dreyfus is a traitor, all Jews are traitors. If a Karl Marx—despite his childhood baptism—is a Jew, all Jews are revolutionaries. If a Jew lends money, all Jews are usurers. If one Jew is a participant in a financial scandal, the Jews are manipulating the economy. Because he is identified as a Jew, the Jew captures attention. There are Jews everywhere. We can be blamed for everything.

Because we Jews are uniquely vulnerable, I believe we can win only brief respite from persecution in a society in which encounters are settled by power. As a Jew, therefore, concerned with my own survival and the survival of the Jews—the two being inextricably linked—I want restraints placed on power. The restraints that matter most to me are those which ensure that I cannot be squashed by power, unnoticed by the rest of the world. If I am in danger, I want to cry out to my fellow Jews and to all those I may be able to enlist as my allies. I want to appeal to the world's sense of justice. I want restraints which prohibit those in power from interfering with my right to speak, my right to publish, or my right to gather with others who also feel threatened. Those in power must not be allowed to prevent us from assembling and joining our voices together so we can speak louder and make sure that we are heard. To defend myself, I must restrain power with freedom, even if the temporary beneficiaries are the enemies of freedom.

Albert Camus said, "Freedom is the concern of the oppressed, and her natural protectors have always come from among the oppressed." It is a matter of self-interest. The oppressed are the victims of power. If they are to end their oppression, they must either win freedom or take power themselves. Many of those who have suffered oppression prefer to take power themselves. One-fifth of all the Jews in the world have sought refuge in their own homeland, Israel. It is a place where Jews hope their oppression will end because there, they make the rules. They have the power. Some Jews have sought refuge in other countries, in scattered communities where most of their neighbors are also Jews. Because Jews loom large in the population of a town such as Skokie, it is also a place where they hope their oppression will end because they can make the rules and exercise the power there. Skokie, in that sense, is a microcosmic reflection of Israel. It is a place where the Jews believe they should be able to defend themselves against invasion.

Only heroic efforts have enabled Israel to resist invasion and to survive contests of power with hostile neighbors. Even those most determined to vindicate Israel's interests through displays of force must know that it is only a question of time until that will no longer suffice to preserve Israel against destruction. Israel requires restraints on the power of its neighbors before it is too late. The sword alone will not ensure the survival of Israel.

Other refuges for the Jews, such as Skokie, have far tinier chances for survival in contests based solely on the exercise of power. Skokie cannot be an independent nation. It is governed by the laws and practices of the state of Illinois and of the United States of America. Seventy thousand people, many of them commuters to Chicago, cannot build a wall around themselves to keep out threatening ideas. Skokie requires other protections. Jews and friends of Jews may hold power in Skokie, but they do not hold power in the rest of the country. Nor will they ever. The Jews in Skokie require restraints on power to guard themselves. Keeping a few Nazis off the streets of Skokie will serve Jews poorly if it means that the freedoms to speak, publish, or assemble any place in the United States are thereby weakened.

In Robert Bolt's play *A Man for All Seasons*, Sir Thomas More asks Roper, "What would you do? Cut a great road through law to get after the devil?" Roper answers, "I'd cut down every law in England to do that." "Oh?" says More. "And when the last law was down and the devil turned around on you—where would you hide, Roper, the laws all being flat? . . . D'you really think you could stand upright in the wind that would blow then? Yes, I'd give the devil benefit of law for my own safety's sake."

Jews cannot hide from the Nazis in Skokie. For their own safety's sake, they must give the devil—the Nazis—benefit of law. It is dangerous to let the Nazis have their say. But it is more dangerous by far to destroy the laws that deny anyone the power to silence Jews if Jews should need to cry out to each other and to the world for succor. Jews have been persecuted too many times in history for anyone to assert that their sufferings are at an end. When the time comes for Jews to speak, to publish, and to march in behalf of their own safety, Illinois and the United States must not be allowed to interfere. The Nazis, I respond to those who ask how I, a Jew, can defend freedom for Nazis, must be free to speak because Jews must be free to speak and because I must be free to speak.

I received many thousands of letters of denunciation. By contrast, there were only a few hundred letters of support. As in the case of the woman who loves free speech more than she detests Nazis, not all the letters of support were entirely reassuring. But some of the support made up for the bitter attacks. One of my favorites was a letter from a doctor in New York City who expressed a strong commitment to the defense of free speech for the Nazis. "I defend the right to express all or any unpopular opinions," said the doctor, "but, as my grandfather would say, they should only drop dead."

The Nazis never marched in Skokie. They announced that march in a successful effort to maintain their visibility during a period when they were prevented from holding demonstrations in Marquette Park, the section of Chicago where they make their headquarters and enjoy the greatest support. The legal battle against the restrictions on free speech in Marquette Park was fought with little public notice at the same time that the highly publicized struggle over Skokie was underway. Just a few days before the Skokie march was scheduled to take place in June 1978, the legal obstacles to demonstrations in Marquette Park were cleared away. Having achieved their original goal, the Nazis cancelled the Skokie march. As they knew very well, if they had gone forward with it, they would have looked ridiculous. The Nazis might have mustered twenty or thirty people to take part in their march while some fifty thousand people were scheduled to participate in a giant counterdemonstration organized by leaders of Skokie's community of concentration-camp survivors.

Even though the Skokie march never took place, Skokie remains the symbolic battleground. During the fifteen months between the time the Nazis first announced their intention to march in Skokie and the time they called off their march after their legal right to hold it was upheld, it was the subject of a great public debate. That debate continues. Almost every daily newspaper in the country published editorials about Skokie. With a few exceptions, the press sided with the American Civil Liberties Union in defending free speech. Letters-to-the-editor columns were heavily weighted on the other side. Syndicated columnists seemed to divide about equally. Skokie has been an inflammatory issue on hundreds of call-in radio shows around the country. It has been a leading topic of sermons in churches and synagogues. United States Senators have stated their views in the *Congressional Record*. Skokie has provoked fierce debates in schools, offices, community centers, old-age homes, restaurants, living rooms, and wherever else people gather. In the debates I heard, almost everyone said they were for free speech. The questions that divided people are whether American Nazis have forfeited their right to speak by identifying themselves with an ideology that produced the Holocaust. And even if the Nazis should be allowed to speak, they could be banned, couldn't they, from a town that is a haven for victims of Nazism? The debates I heard were rarely calm. Many were dominated by intense emotional outbursts. In some cases, it seemed as though the bitterness expressed would do permanent damage to relationships between people.

Why has Skokie become a symbol and a rallying point? The Nazi attempt to march in Skokie, Illinois, raised no novel legal questions. The arguments for and against free speech in Skokie are identical to those in hundreds of other court cases. Nor, regrettably, is there anything novel in the spectacle of a group of Americans who choose to strut in storm-trooper uniforms with swastika armbands. In the past two decades, such sights have become a familiar part of the urban landscape. The Nazis have no more adherents today and represent no greater a political threat today than during any part of that period. Nor is there anything unusual about a Nazi attempt to march in a place where their mere appearance is a calculated insult to the memory of the victims of Nazism. Like many other dissident groups, the Nazis are intentionally provocative, hoping to attract attention and to trap their enemies into ugly and discrediting responses.

Skokie is, nevertheless, a crisis point for American freedom and it will remain a classic case in the annals of law. The emergence of the Skokie case as a cause célèbre lies in part in its timing. Skokie comes at a moment when American Jews fear that they—and Israel—will be betrayed by the Western democracies. Will the need for Arab oil and petrodollars take precedence over Jewish interests? Skokie symbolizes the reemergence of the ultimate threat to Jewish existence. The world stood by and watched the Nazis destroy the Jews. It could happen again.

Skokie also comes at a moment of special fragility in the uneasy alliance between people with a primary commitment to left-wing politics and people with a primary commitment to civil liberties. The civil rights movement of the 1960s and the antiwar movement and opposition to Richard Nixon forged that alliance. Those are all past. Skokie and related cases shattered that alliance.

Finally, Skokie comes at a moment when liberalism is in sharp decline. It is getting difficult to find any candidate for public office willing to identify himself or herself as a liberal. One of the most frequently repeated lines around is the definition of a conservative as "a liberal who has been mugged." Defense of free speech for Nazis in Skokie, many people believe, is a prime example of liberal naiveté, roughly comparable to inviting a mugger home for dinner. Do not defend the enemy.

Whatever the reasons, Skokie has sent shock waves through many American institutions. Jewish organizations and other groups that have tried to maintain their traditional commitment to free speech find themselves out of step with their own constituencies. Some have taken refuge in silence while others discover special circumstances in Skokie which make it different from every other case of a group attempting to express its views in a place where its doctrines are anathema. Even the nation's leading free-speech organization, the American Civil Liberties Union, has watched a substantial part of its own membership quitting in angry protest over the ACLU's defense of the rights of Nazis who want to march in Skokie.

This book tells the story of Skokie and the other recent cases in which the enemies of freedom have claimed for themselves the rights that they would deny to others. It describes the historical roots of these cases. I try to state as best I can the arguments of those who would limit the right to speak of groups such as the Nazis and the Ku Klux Klan. I also attempt to answer those arguments. And the book assesses the impact of Skokie on the people and institutions that helped to shape the case and were, in turn, shaped by it.

1

Understanding Media

On August 25, 1967, John Patler shot and killed George Lincoln Rockwell in a shopping center in Arlington, Virginia. Patler, a follower of Rockwell and a former captain in the American Nazi Party, had been ejected some time earlier for stirring up dissension within the party.

Rockwell's murder deprived the post-World War II Nazi movement in the United States of its principal organizer and of its only charismatic figure. Through his flair for attracting attention, Rockwell had fostered the illusion that Nazism had reemerged in the United States with all the strength it had achieved a generation earlier in the days of the Bund.

Before the United States entered World War II, a large and well-organized Nazi movement existed in the United States. The German American Bund was capable of assembling 3,500 people in the Yorkville Casino on the upper East Side of New York to celebrate Hitler's forty-ninth birthday in 1938. Bund-operated summer camps appeared to be a mechanism for training a domestic version of the Hitler Youth. The fortunes of the Bund began a rapid decline in

11

1940 after Hitler and Stalin signed their nonaggression pact. During 1940 and 1941 it became increasingly evident that the United States would be drawn into the war against the Axis powers. The imprisonment of the Bund's leader, Fritz Kuhn, a German-born chemist employed by the Ford Motor Company, also contributed to the decline. He was convicted of stealing funds from the Bund.

While pro-Nazi sentiment among some Bund adherents undoubtedly persisted throughout the war years, their organization disappeared, not to appear again after the conclusion of the war. There was no declared Nazi movement in the United States until the emergence of George Lincoln Rockwell more than a decade after the end of the war.

Rockwell was tall and handsome and had a commanding presence. He also had a sense of drama and he knew how to exploit the shock and dread that his public appearances provoked. Rockwell obtained especially generous helpings of publicity on the frequent occasions when he would apply for permits for street rallies. Public officials habitually would turn him down and, in the process, denounce him. New York City's Mayor Robert F. Wagner rejected one such request for a permit, an application to hold a demonstration in Union Square Park on July 4, 1960, saying it was "an invitation to riot and disorder from a halfpenny Hitler." The courts eventually ordered the New York City parks department to give Rockwell his permit. Each step of the proceedings provided publicity for Rockwell.

In his travels around the country to picket showings of the movie *Exodus*, Rockwell never could gather more than a handful of fellow pickets. Yet the calculated outrage was always effective in winning headlines. Nazis showed up at a Republican Party meeting with signs saying "Save Ike from the Kikes," and a lone Nazi paraded in blackface at a Democratic convention with a sign reading "I's the Mississippi delegate."

Rockwell understood instinctively the theories Marshall

McLuhan would propound a few years later in *Understanding Media*. A couple of Nazis in full regalia would get far more attention from the media of visual communications than a large and well-organized national movement provided that they chose the targets for their demonstrations shrewdly.

During the ten or eleven years during which Rockwell led the Nazi movement in the United States, he created the impression that he led a sizable organization. At its peak in the early sixties, however, there were never more than about 400 or 500 members of or contributors to his American Nazi Party throughout the country. A few rival Nazi groups, such as the National Renaissance Party in New York, had some 200 to 300 members among them.

The leader of the National Renaissance Party was James Madole, a cadaverous-looking middle-aged man who lived with his mother and was accompanied by her wherever he went. Madole and Rockwell both were summoned to appear at a hearing in early 1967 of a New York State legislative committee investigating right-wing political activities in the New York City police department. While there was no evidence that either Rockwell or Madole had followers in the department, their appearance at the hearing ensured that the legislators themselves would get publicity. To aid their own political careers by portraying themselves as anti-Nazi, the legislators who arranged the hearing were entirely willing to give the Nazis the visibility they also craved.

Rockwell and Madole both called the New York Civil Liberties Union for assistance, and I went to the hearing flanked by the two rival "führers." Neither Madole nor Rockwell said a word to the other. As I stood between them, they stared at each other right past me with an intensity it is difficult to forget.

At the time of Rockwell's death his organization, which he had renamed the National Socialist White People's Party, was in decline. Rumor had it that Rockwell and his storm troopers had so little money that occasionally they made do with canned dog food in the party headquarters that was also their home in Arlington, Virginia.

After Rockwell's death, he was succeeded by Matt Koehl, a former follower of Madole and the National Renaissance Party and before that, a founder of another such group, the National States Rights Party. Koehl, who had been active in similar fringe groups since he was in high school, lacked Rockwell's public personality and capacity for leadership. He did claim, however, that Rockwell had left a will bequeathing leadership of the Nazis to him. Koehl's causes and slogans—"Free Rudolf Hess" was one of them—evoked little excitement and the party splintered. Rockwell lieutenants established several new "national" parties in cities around the country. Despite their "national" names, they generally operate only locally.

Koehl's National Socialist White People's Party, still based in Arlington, remains the largest Nazi organization in the country. It has about a hundred members and several times that number of "supporters." The NSWPP publishes a monthly newspaper, *White Power*. About 10,000 copies of each issue are printed, most of them for free distribution. Koehl would like the party to become more respectable and to run candidates in elections. The founder, Rockwell, ran for governor of Virginia in 1965 and a few persons associated with NSWPP have campaigned for local offices in recent years. In instances when they have gotten on the ballot in cities such as Baltimore, Milwaukee, St. Louis, and San Francisco, the NSWPP candidates have secured as much as 5 percent or 6 percent of the vote.

The Nazis won more electoral support in Milwaukee than anywhere else in the United States. Nazi leaflets began turning up in Milwaukee schools in the fall of 1974. The leaflets were the product of a local group affiliated with the National Socialist White People's Party. During 1975, NSWPP organized several demonstrations in Milwaukee, including one in front of the Milwaukee Jewish Community Center. The event that attracted the largest amount of publicity to the Nazis was their establishment of a booth at the Wisconsin State Fair in Milwaukee featuring photographs of George Lincoln Rockwell and a banner which read, "AMERICA AWAKE! DETENTE IS A TRAGIC MISTAKE." Among the several young Nazis in storm-trooper uniforms with swastika emblems who attended the booth was Arthur Jones, a Vietnam veteran and a former student at the University of Wisconsin. A year later, Jones announced his candidacy for mayor of Milwaukee. He filed close to two thousand signatures to get on the ballot and conducted a campaign with paid advertisements in newspapers, on radio, and on television. He ran fourth in the primary with about five thousand votes.

As a result of the Nazi activity, the Milwaukee County Board of Supervisors adopted an ordinance in 1976 banning group defamation on county property. A similar ordinance proposed in the Milwaukee City Council to apply to city property was defeated. While many Jewish organizations supported these ordinances, the Wisconsin Civil Liberties Union opposed their adoption, finding strong allies in the Jewish community, among them the Milwaukee Anti-Defamation League and the Milwaukee Jewish Council. Robert Freibert, an attorney prominent in Jewish affairs in Milwaukee, described the group defamation ordinance in the *Wisconsin Jewish Chronicle* as a "wretched piece of legislation." "The specter of the Nazis is a disgusting specter," he said, "but do we throw out everything we believe in to go after one group? We do ourselves a tremendous injustice if we support this ordinance."

The NSWPP has some ties to Nazi groups in other countries through a federating group known as the World Union of National Socialists that was founded by Rockwell. While this group exists largely on paper and in the fantasies of Koehl and his associates, it proved real enough to stage a welcome for Koehl on a 1975 visit to Germany. The reception was organized by a Hitler-era Luftwaffe fighter pilot who continues to profess Nazi views.

The other dozen or so Nazi groups in the United States are much smaller than the National Socialist White People's Party. They range from a tiny but relatively affluent group based in Reedy, West Virginia, financed by a businessman and post-World War II immigrant, George P. Dietz, whose father was a member of the SS in Germany, to a group in Los Angeles that has declared itself America's first homosexual Nazi organization. The Los Angeles group, the National Socialist League, holds its "conventions" in gay bars. It is regarded by other Nazi organizations as a fake intended to discredit their movement. Quarrels within the Nazi organizations are often settled violently. In one such dispute, Joe Tomasi, a West Coast Nazi leader and probably the most charismatic of Rockwell's followers, was shot dead in 1975.

The Nazi organization that has captured the limelight in the past two years, however, is the National Socialist Party of America. Its twenty-five or thirty members gather in brown-shirted uniforms with black boots at their party's headquarters, Rockwell Hall, a storefront on the southwest side of Chicago. Francis Joseph (Frank) Collin, the party's leader, who lives upstairs above the Chicago storefront with his German shepherd dog and two of the storm troopers, devotes full time to his party. The National Socialist Party of America also has some followers in Missouri, Texas, and California.

Jerry McGhee, the chairman of the Chicago unit of the National Socialist White People's Party, and his organization have no use for Frank Collin. "We may have the same philosophy," says McGhee, "but we do not condone his tactics. He's violent. We believe in working with the law." Collin is distrusted also by other Nazi groups around the country because he is apparently of Jewish descent on one side.

Despite Frank Collin's vigorous denials, it seems likely that his father, Max Collin, is a Jew who survived imprisonment for three months in the concentration camp at Dachau. Max Collin, who seems to have changed his name from Max Cohn in 1946, apparently never sees his son. Frank Collin's mother is not Jewish and he was reared a Catholic.

If the allegation is true that Frank Collin is the son of a Jew, he would not be the first American Nazi with such origins. In 1967, a reporter for the *New York Times* discovered that a Nazi activist in New York State had been born a Jew. When the Nazi was interviewed, he threatened to kill himself if the *Times* exposed his ancestry. The *Times* published the story and the Nazi committed suicide.

Frank Collin became a member of George Lincoln Rockwell's American Nazi Party in 1965. Some time after Rockwell's death he broke with what had become the National Socialist White People's Party. Collin says the break took place at his initiative because the NSWPP was ineffectual and its officers "scum." Collin's former colleagues at the NSWPP say they forced him out because they discovered his Jewish origins, and they have derisively offered a large cash reward to anyone who can prove that Collin is not a Jew. They also accuse Collin of taking party funds to start his own organization in Chicago.

Of the current generation of Nazis, Frank Collin comes closest to George Lincoln Rockwell in demonstrating flair and leadership. He does not have Rockwell's physically prepossessing appearance; his Hitler haircut looks ridiculous. But his public statements are fierce. "My life is a bullet," he says, "aimed at the enemy." And, when asked how he became a Nazi, he likes to tell people that as a child he saw an anti-Nazi film on television sponsored by the Anti-Defamation League. The film included sequences showing Hitler.

"I saw a great man," Collins says, "a man deeply committed to something very powerful. I've loved Hitler ever since."

The southwest Chicago neighborhood of Marquette Park where Rockwell Hall is located has modest and neat one-family homes. The streets are lined with trees and the lawns carefully tended. Most of the residents are blue-collar workers whose families came from Eastern Europe. Marquette Park is all-white. It is also the choice of blacks living nearby who seek escape from their crowded ghettos. Marquette Park's racial segregation has become a major issue. A message painted on the side of Rockwell Hall expresses the dominant response of the white residents of Marquette Park. "Nigger Go Home," it reads. That message, and a variation that says "NIGGERS BEWARE! Marquette Park Stays White," turn up on many of the placards carried by white teenagers in demonstrations. Some of those placards are illustrated with swastikas.

During 1976 and 1977, blacks made several attempts to demonstrate in the park that gives the area its name and on the public sidewalks nearby. Some of their demonstrations were stopped by neighborhood teenagers, some by the police. On one occasion, the Martin Luther King, Jr. Movement Coalition got a permit to hold a parade. A large contingent of police was supposed to be on hand to give them protection. When members of the coalition showed up for their parade, a relatively small number of police were on hand. A coalition leader had telephoned the night before and cancelled the demonstration, the police said. They didn't have enough officers to guard the march and it couldn't be held. When some members of the coalition attempted to proceed with their march, the police arrested the marchers. That did not prevent Marquette Park's white teenagers from responding with a small-scale riot. Several police officers were injured. Another time, an off-duty corrections officer was shot during an anti-black riot by Marquette Park teenagers.

The racial tensions of Marquette Park provide fertile soil for Frank Collin to plow. It is a bit surprising, therefore, that his National Socialist Party of America has not grown significantly. Despite all the press attention he has received, Collin's organization remains minuscule. And, perhaps because of mistrust based on the reports of Jewish ancestry, Collin has been unable to unite the Nazi organizations throughout the country under his leadership. They remain as fragmented and as hostile to each other as they ever have been in the more than a decade that has elapsed since George Lincoln Rockwell's death.

While there is no evidence of organizational connection between the Nazis and the Ku Klux Klan, some of the people attracted to these groups occasionally shift allegiances among them. Photographs appearing in newspapers around the country at the time of the Chicago Seven trial in 1969 showed a lone man in a Nazi uniform picketing the federal courthouse where the trial was taking place. This was David Duke, now leader of the Knights of the Ku Klux Klan.

Based in Metairie, Louisiana, Duke's group is one of a dozen or more organizations in the country using the Klan name. Like the Nazis, the various Klan organizations have little to do with each other. Much of their time is spent in conducting internal feuds. The natural tendency of all radical political groups to preoccupy themselves with internecine warfare is, no doubt, exacerbated in the case of Klan organizations by their extensive infiltration by undercover law-enforcement agents. This is a legacy of the violent role of several Klan organizations in resisting the civil rights movement of the 1960s. It made any group calling itself the Klan a major target for FBI surveillance and penetration.

David Duke's Klan organization appears to be a little larger than Frank Collin's National Socialist Party of America. It is, nevertheless, a minuscule organization. Other Klan organizations are a good deal larger. Like Collin, however,

Duke has obtained publicity all out of proportion to the size of his movement. In a letter to his followers celebrating the accomplishments of 1977, Duke boasted, "This year I have appeared on approximately 225 radio and television programs delivering our vital message to over 90 million. This includes only those who have heard my talk shows and does not count those millions more who have read newspapers and magazine articles and who have heard radio and television news reports about our activities."

Duke was exaggerating, but he has gotten a lot of attention. So far, however, he has been unable to translate the publicity he has obtained into organizational growth. The older and more staid Klan groups that lack charismatic leaders still have more members.

As for Nazism, is it resurgent in the United States? How dangerous are these bands that parade in uniform and hate each other as much as they hate anyone else? The American Jewish Committee, which keeps a close watch on anti-Semitic groups in the United States, published a report in November 1977 on "American Nazis—Myth or Menace?" The report's survey of the Nazi organizations finds them politically ineffectual. "If, as the desperate Nazi groups maintain, their ultimate objective is to become the dominant political power," says the report, written by Milton Ellerin of the American Jewish Committee's staff, "they manifest an abysmal ignorance of what motivates the American electorate. American Nazism has failed to develop a motivating philosophy or attract a political figure of stature to its cause. Neither Rockwell nor any of the current array of would-be leaders have blueprinted a platform that realistically addresses itself to the concerns of blue-collar workers or the middle class, their only sources of recruits to date. No Nazi has addressed himself to the problem of inflation, unemployment, the quality of life, crime in the streets, environment, taxes, wages, or foreign policy." The Anti-Defamation

League, which also monitors such groups, seconded this view in a March 1978 report. "The American Nazi movement," said the ADL, "is politically impotent, capable and noteworthy only in the production of vicious hate propaganda, occasional street violence, and troublemaking on the local level. Often boisterously visible, its nationwide network of no more than 1,000 to 1,200 members—in a country of 217 million—makes it clear that its visibility is far out of proportion to its numbers."

The American Jewish Committee's report notes that a recent Nazi publication was candid enough to acknowledge that "the supporters we do have include all manner of dead beats, police informers, regalia freaks, dilettantes and dabblers, right-wing kooks, religious nuts, anarchists, and nihilists." Assessing the movement, the American Jewish Committee report finds: "The danger of American Nazism then is not that it has the capacity to engulf Americans or influence our government and its institutions."

The Anti-Defamation League and the American Jewish Committee assertions that the Nazis are politically impotent do not mean that the organizations see no danger in the Nazi movement. The ADL says that the Nazis have "a potential for generating temporary local passions out of local tensions and for creating occasional disturbances, often with tragic consequences." And, the AJC points out, while the Nazis will not take over the government of the United States, they are capable of cruelty and violence against individuals. A bizarre incident in Chicago in May 1977 made that clear. Raymond Schultz, a Nazi, murdered Sydney Cohen, a Jew, by forcing Cohen to inhale hydrogen cyanide. This was the poison used by the Nazis to kill Jews in the death camps in Germany and in Eastern Europe. When Schultz was arrested, he killed himself by the same method while in policy custody. A police investigation later discovered evidence that Schultz had assembled a large collection of poisonous chemicals, bomb parts, and ammunition and that he had compiled a list of prominent Chicago Jews who were to be targets for murder. Several months before this incident, a Nazi follower in New Rochelle, New York, Frederick Cowan, had gone on a rampage and killed five people before shooting and killing himself. In December 1977, several of Frank Collin's followers were indicted for attempted murder following a violent confrontation between Nazis and Jewish Defense League members outside a hotel in Chicago where an Israel bonds dinner was underway. A seventeen-year-old young man in Charlotte, North Carolina, fired shots into a crowd of blacks attending a 1977 Labor Day picnic. One person was killed and three were injured. The young man then killed himself. Police in Charlotte said the youth was a Nazi. "The concern," says the American Jewish Committee, "is and should be with [Nazism's] harmful effects on emotionally unstable or zealous adherents who act on the built-up hatreds it inspires. That is a danger for all Americans to think about."

2

"Never Again"

"What preserves the Jew's separateness," says historian Peter Gay, "is far less his ancient religion or some distinct culture than his terrible memories; it is Hitler who has defined the modern Jew and continues to define him from the grave."

To this, it must be added that while the Holocaust was the worst episode in the long history of the Jews and, very likely, in the history of civilized society, to many Jews it does not represent a sharp break with the rest of their experiences in the Diaspora. The Holocaust is, rather, the culmination of 1,900 years in which to be a Jew was to be a target for hate, oppression, and murder. The origins of Auschwitz are in the portrayals of Jews as Christ-killers; in the accusations that first appeared in England in the twelfth century that Jews committed ritual murders for Passover; in the expulsion of the Jews from England, France, Spain, Portugal, and other European countries; in the Spanish Inquisition that burned Jews at the stake for three and a half centuries and claimed its last victim as late as 1826; * in the pogroms that regularly punctuated life in the Jewish Pale of Eastern Europe; and in the fraudulent Protocols of the Elders of Zion published by the Okhrana, the secret police of tsarist Russia. It is not just that Auschwitz could happen again. It happened before many times, if on a smaller scale. Who, then, is to say that Auschwitz was the last time? If Nazis proclaim their doctrines in Skokie, Illinois, haven for thousands of Holocaust survivors, isn't it happening again?

Jews in the United States and elsewhere have derived several great lessons from the Holocaust. One lesson is that refinement and culture are no guarantee against the horrors of the extermination camps. The people of Goethe, Schiller, and Mozart could be more brutal than Ukrainian peasants caught up in the frenzy of a pogrom. Another lesson is that the assimilated Jews of Germany, Holland, and France could become victims as readily as the Jews who lived apart in the *shtetls* in Eastern Europe. Another lesson, and perhaps the most important, is that resistance is essential.

That cultured Germans could commit such great evils makes Jews fear that they enjoy no safety anywhere, even in the United States. Signs of anti-Semitism in this country, therefore, are cause for great alarm. Many things that might seem trivial in isolation—a statement by a member of the Joint Chiefs of Staff that American foreign policy is subject to undue Jewish influence; a black poet's suggestive line about Jewish store owners in Harlem; an "affirmative action" program, designed to benefit racial minorities, that Jews see as a new *numerus clausus*: an angry outburst by an actress

* Cecil Roth, the great Oxford University historian of the Jews, reported in his book *The Spanish Inquisition* that in 1826, "Public opinion was no longer capable of supporting the idea of a public burning." Instead, a teacher was garrotted and "the body was encased in a barrel on which scarlet flames were painted so that the traditional penalty might be carried out symbolically at least." In earlier times, the Inquisition was not so delicate. A one-time Secretary of the Holy Office wrote a history in 1808 in which he calculated that, in Spain alone, the Inquisition burned at the stake 31,912 persons.

against "Zionist hoodlums"—are ominous in the light of the history of the Jews. How much more frightening, therefore, to see American Nazis in uniform strutting near Jewish homes!

Ever since the second half of the eighteenth century many Jews in Europe believed that assimilation was the solution to the age-old problem of mistreatment of Jews. The idea of assimilation is linked inextricably with the name of Moses Mendelssohn. Born in Dessau in 1729, Mendelssohn followed his rabbi to Berlin in 1743. At the gates of Berlin, he had to pay the *Leibzoll*, the special tax imposed on Jews. In Berlin, Mendelssohn acquired fame and exemption from taxes as a *Schutzjude* (protected Jew) by publishing philosophical treatises. They were written in German —this itself was considered remarkable for a Jew—and they were renowned for their brilliance. One of Mendelssohn's essays was chosen over the work of Immanuel Kant for a prize in metaphysics given out by the Berlin Academy of Sciences. For the last twenty years of his life, Mendelssohn was known as "the German Socrates." He was the model for Lessing's *Nathan the Wise*. German Jews celebrated him in a line I often heard from my father: "From Moses [the prophet and lawgiver] to Moses [Maimonides, the twelfth-century philosopher] to Moses [Mendelssohn], there was none like Moses."

Mendelssohn was a pioneer among Jews in the use of the German language and in the rediscovery of Hebrew, the two component parts of the language previously spoken by Jews in Germany and Eastern Europe. Mendelssohn remained a Jew, wrote essays on Judaism, translated portions of the Old Testament into German, published a weekly paper in Hebrew, and was a vigorous advocate of Jewish civil rights. His influence, however, was to make many Jews attempt to abandon their separate identities as Jews and Judaism itself. Several of his children and grandchildren— such as Felix Mendelssohn, the composer—became Christians. Moses Mendelssohn went over to the dominant culture and some of his family and followers went over to the dominant religion.

The Nazis in Germany did not distinguish between Jews who converted to Christianity and Jews who remained Jews. In this sense, Nazism represented a break with most of the previous history of anti-Jewish prejudice. Earlier, it was the separate religion of the Jews that was the target. Under the Nuremberg laws, anyone of Jewish descent became a victim. The assimilation of the Jews in Germany that had proceeded so far between the 1760s and the 1930s proved no protection at all.

Theodor Herzl, an assimilated Jew born in Budapest in 1860, was one of the first to understand that anti-Jewish sentiment was undergoing a transformation from religious to racial bias. Herzl had been an advocate of the baptism of all Jewish children as a solution to the Jewish question. His views changed radically, however, when he covered the trial of Captain Alfred Dreyfus in Paris in 1894 as a journalist writing for the *Neue Freie Presse*. That Captain Dreyfus was a fully assimilated Jew did not spare him from anti-Jewish bias. Since the bias was racial, and not religious, and since a race cannot convert, Herzl decided that the only protection for the Jews was a homeland of their own. He became a fervent advocate of the creation of a Jewish state and is regarded today as the father of the Zionist movement and of the state of Israel.

The strong ties most assimilated American Jews feel to the state of Israel is a source of some wonder to many non-Jews. Non-Jews might find it even more surprising to discover that pro-Israel sentiment is often far stronger among Jews with virtually no religious ties to Judaism than among some of the most Orthodox Jewish sects. But what Herzl saw at the Dreyfus trial was made manifest to Jews all over the world by the Holocaust: no matter how they conduct their lives, the rest of the world regards them as a race apart because they are Jews. Their fate, therefore, is linked to the fate of Jews all over the world and, especially, to the fate of Israel.

Israel became the refuge for most of the half million or so Jews who survived World War II in German-occupied Europe. The next largest number, about 100,000, made their way to the United States. They are people who managed to live by hiding in the woods, or in cellars, or by escaping with false identity papers. Few survived the greatest killing center in human history, Auschwitz. A few more survived camps like Belzec, Bergen-Belsen, Buchenwald, Chelmno, Dachau, Maidanek, Matthausen, Nordhausen, Ravensbrueck, Sachsenhausen, Sobibor, Theresienstadt, and Treblinka. Only about 75,000 of the millions of Jews who went into the camps came out alive. Now, thirty-three years after the end of the war, the survivors are getting on in years and their number is dwindling. A few hundred death camp survivors came to Skokie, Illinois. Seven thousand of the town's residents are Jews from German-occupied Europe and members of their families.

Outside of New York City, Skokie is one of the largest survivor communities in the United States. Settlement there was not by design. It just happened. One of the survivors, Mrs. Erna Gans, now chairman of the Skokie Youth Commission, says, "We lost all our families. We have no one else. One person would marry and move here, and then another. And another. We don't even explain it. We just keep in touch." The survivors have terrible memories. One man who came to Skokie in 1951 is a survivor of Auschwitz and Maidanek. His wife, whom he met after the war, survived Bergen-Belsen. Most of his family died in the Warsaw ghetto. In Maidanek he recalls seeing an SS man shove a poker hot from the fire down a young boy's throat until the boy was dead. Another man saw a concentration camp guard smash a rifle butt in his young daughter's face, kick his wife in the stomach, and lead them both to the gas chamber. Another man's mother was buried alive when she and other residents of a town in Lithuania were thrown into a well and dirt and gravel were poured in over them.

The resistance of Skokie's Jews to a proposed demonstration in their town by American Nazis was a kind of delayed response of anger about the past. When German Nazis overran their towns in Eastern Europe, most Jews had not resisted. They remembered the few efforts to resist the pogroms in Russia in the early part of the century; the pogroms simply grew in fury. The 1938 killing of an official of the German embassy in Paris by a young Jew, Herschel Grynszpan, protesting the deportation of his parents and thousands of other Jews from their homes in Germany to Poland, led to *Kristallnacht*, November 9, 1938. Virtually all of the six hundred synagogues in Germany, some of them ancient buildings, and thousands of Jewish businesses and homes were destroyed in one night. Tens of thousands of Jews were rounded up and thrown in concentration camps. Hundreds died that night. A fine of one billion marks was imposed on the Jews of the Reich as compensation for Grynszpan's crime and a decree issued transferring Jewish businesses to "Aryan" control.

Jews in Europe lacked arms to fight the well-equipped German army. And they did not know, and could not know, what their fate would be in the camps. Resistance seemed like madness. Today, remembering, and with the example of Israel's resistance to PLO terror, not to resist seems like madness. "I will not be a sheep again," says a Bergen-Belsen survivor who now lives in Skokie.

Inevitably, the survivors have been affected by a controversy brought to the surface in the United States by the publication of Hannah Arendt's 1963 book, *Eichmann in Jerusalem*. It provoked both intense discussion of the need for resistance and recriminations about cooperation between Jewish community leaders in Europe and the Nazis. The story had been known previously, was widely discussed in Israel, and had been recounted in exhaustive detail in Raul Hilberg's monumental book published in 1961, *The Destruction of the European Jews.* But Dr. Arendt's book, appearing first in serial form in *The New Yorker*, made Jewish cooperation in their own extermination a subject of popular discussion in this country.

> *Jewish officials [said Arendt] could be trusted to compile the lists of persons and of their property, to secure money from the deportees to defray the expenses of their deportation and extermination, to keep track of vacated apartments, to supply police forces to help seize Jews and get them on trains, until, as a last gesture, they handed over the assets of the Jewish community in good order for final confiscation. They distributed the Yellow Star badges. . . . The well-known fact that the actual work of killing in the extermination centers was usually in the hands of Jewish commandos had been fairly and squarely established by witnesses for the prosecution— how they had worked in the gas chambers and the crematories, how they had pulled the gold teeth and cut the hair of the corpses, how they had dug the graves and, later, dug them up again to extinguish the traces of mass murder; how Jewish technicians had built gas chambers in Theresienstadt, where the Jewish "autonomy" had been carried so far that even the hangman was a Jew.*

There were fierce attacks on Arendt's book, many of them based on the view that she was blaming the victims of the Holocaust for their extermination. Her purpose, as she made plain in the book, was to demonstrate that hardly any of the voices that should have been raised in moral protest against Nazism were to be heard in Germany or the territories conquered by the Reich. Where political and religious leaders did speak out against the Nazis, notably in a country such as Denmark, most Jews were saved. Those Jews who died, and those Jews who cooperated with the Nazis in the belief that they were making things easier for other Jews, were victims of the silence of Europe's moral leadership as they were victims of the Nazis.

The reaction to Hannah Arendt's book helped to focus attention on the Jews in the ghettos of Bialystok, Warsaw, Vilna, and a few other places who participated in heroic, if futile, uprisings against the Nazis. By the mid-1960s, American Jews shared the view prevalent earlier in Israel: Jews must confront, resist, and beat back every manifestation of anti-Jewish prejudice. Later in the 1960s and in the 1970s, Israel's successes in its periodic wars with neighboring Arab states hardened that view. Israel is living proof to American Jews of the effectiveness of resistance.

In the early 1960s, Jewish organizations in the United States debated what they should do about George Lincoln Rockwell's provocative demonstrations. The consensus was reflected in a resolution adopted in 1962 by the National Jewish Community Relations Advisory Council, a coordinating group presently comprising nine major national Jewish organizations and 103 local Jewish community groups. The 1962 resolution flatly opposed all prior restraints. And in 1963 the NJCRAC said that "public protests against [Rockwell's] appearances and noisy or violent mass demonstrations merely provide him with increased publicity and bolster the image of martyred hero which has such an appeal to the elements he seeks to attract to his banner."

The change in the views of the leadership of Jewish organizations was reflected in a January 1978 speech to a meeting of the National Jewish Community Relations Advisory Council by the group's national chairman, Theodore R. Mann. A distinguished Philadelphia attorney with a strong commitment to civil liberties, Mann told his colleagues in the NJCRAC that "I am troubled by our 1963 conclusion that public protests against Nazi appearances merely provide them with increased publicity and bolster their image of martyred heroes. It seems to me curiously outdated. . . . We are attempting to teach the lessons of the Holocaust to our non-Jewish neighbors. . . . If we cannot stop Nazi appearances, if we must endure the anguish, must we not use every possible means to fasten the general public's attention onto the principles for which these Nazis stand? In most cases, creative Jewish leadership should be able to fashion a counterdemonstration or protest march or meeting, with signs and literature and releases to the media depicting the bestial acts of Nazi Germany, which would provide both an outlet for Jewish anguish and a lesson for our neighbors as to what the swastika really means."

Mann concluded his address with a plea to the NJCRAC not to abandon its opposition to all prior restraints. Other Jewish leaders did not see it that way. The national governing council of the American Jewish Congress, one of the constituent bodies of the NJCRAC, adopted a resolution in January 1978 calling for prior restraint. "We believe," said the Congress, "that the courts may and should prohibit the National Socialist Party of America [the Nazi Party] from marching through Skokie, Illinois."

In the early 1960s, at the time of the Rockwell demonstrations, the American Jewish Congress had been a leading voice in the Jewish community for First Amendment freedoms. By 1978, it was one of the loudest opponents of the ACLU, announcing that it would file a brief in the U.S. Supreme Court in support of prior restraint if the high court agreed to review the Skokie case. Most other major national Jewish organizations also supported prior restraint in Skokie. Some, such as the American Jewish Committee, arrived at that position only after prolonged internal debate and, when they adopted resolutions, tried to limit them as much as possible to the circumstances of Skokie. Other groups, such as the Anti-Defamation League, were willing to impose much broader restrictions on speech.

An unacknowledged but important factor in the deliberations of the major Jewish organizations was the radical Jewish Defense League, a small group, founded in 1968 by Rabbi Meir Kahane, regarded with contempt by many Jewish leaders. Several years ago, JDL members were implicated in a number of violent protests against treatment of the Jews in Russia, among them the bombings in 1971 of the Glen Cove, Long Island, mansion owned by the Soviet Union mission to the United Nations, the Amtorg Soviet trade office in New York, and the offices of impresario Sol Hurok. The Hurok office bombing, in which a woman was killed, was in reprisal for Hurok's refusal to cancel appearances in the United States by Russian performing artists. Another series of violent episodes took place in 1976. Four JDL activists are now serving prison sentences for their part in the violence.

Like the Nazis, the JDL knows how to attract attention out of all proportion to the number of its adherents. The JDL now claims a membership of 19,000, up sharply during the year following the first announcement of the Skokie march. The publicity it gets is a product of its militance, its effective use of symbols, and its choice of the times and places of its demonstrations.

The JDL's skill in attracting attention was manifest in several of the demonstrations directed against the ACLU and against me personally. One such demonstration took place in front of the ACLU's national headquarters on April 20, 1978. The date was chosen because the Nazis had planned to march in Skokie that day (though the continuing litigation made the Nazi march impossible) and because it was Hitler's birthday. The leaflet handed out by the JDL in front of the ACLU offices was headed, "HAPPY BIRTHDAY ADOLF." The leaflet went on to say that "Nazis Have No Rights." By distributing it in front of the

offices of the ACLU, which was defending the rights of
Nazis, the JDL had picked exactly the place where its
message would stand out in sharpest relief. The JDL used
symbols effectively by delivering a "present" to the ACLU
intended to imply that we were responsible for the killing
of Jews. The present was a wooden board. A photograph
of a crematorium had been mounted on the board and a
montage had been constructed over the photograph con-
sisting of shards of glass and half a lampshade. Red paint
had been dripped over everything to represent the blood
of the victims of the Holocaust and a small brass plate had
been affixed commemorating Hitler's birthday as the occasion of the gift.

That particular demonstration took place on the public
sidewalk. The JDL's only effort to enter the ACLU offices
was to deliver the present. Several other JDL demonstrations, however, took place inside ACLU offices. On one
occasion, the JDL members arrived with baseball bats. The
demonstrations inside ACLU offices disrupted work. As
Rabbi Kahane told me during the course of one such demonstration in 1977, he would be delighted if I had him
arrested. If the ACLU had been provoked into asking police to arrest demonstrators, the JDL would have gotten a
great deal more publicity than it could otherwise obtain
and its purposes would have been well served.

The Jewish Defense League's two-word slogan—"Never
Again"—speaks volumes. It says that anti-Semitism will
never again go unchallenged. Nazis will never again rise.
The Holocaust will never again happen. Jews will never
again go like sheep to the slaughter. The big Jewish organizations may regard JDL as a bunch of hoodlums, but
every Jew is stirred deeply by the vow of never again. And
every Jewish organization's stand on Skokie has been shaped
by the sense of militancy and resistance that is epitomized
in the JDL slogan.

The major national Jewish groups enjoy far more sophisticated leadership than is available to most other cause organizations in the United States. The leaders of these groups know very well that the Nazi movement in the United States is minuscule, that it has no prospect of gaining a significant number of adherents, and that it represents no political danger. They know also that a tiny Nazi movement serves the purposes of organized Jewry. It is a reminder to Jews of the importance of rallying to the support of Jewish causes. It plays a crucial role in stimulating renewed interest in the Holocaust. It prods organized Christianity to seek ways to demonstrate solidarity with Jews, as in the distribution and wearing of yellow stars at the time a march was scheduled to take place in Skokie. It even makes it more difficult for the shapers of American foreign policy to abandon Israel. Above all, the major Jewish organizations understand that by appearing in the guise that is ugliest to non-Jewish Americans and wearing uniforms against which non-Jews fought a war, Nazi anti-Semitism preempts the field. This much is even conceded by Bonnie Pechter, the young woman who recently replaced Rabbi Kahane as the national leader of the Jewish Defense League. Even though her organization focuses most of its efforts on the Nazis, she told me that she believes the Klan is far more dangerous to Jews because it is homegrown and was not a wartime enemy of the United States. The Nazis deter the expression of anti-Semitism in forms that might be more palatable to the American public and, therefore, more threatening to the Jews. Other anti-Semites must impose restraints on themselves for fear of being bracketed with the almost universally hated Nazis. A strong Nazi movement would be a great danger to Jews in the United States; a weak Nazi movement with no potential for growth has its uses. This lesson is clear to the Jewish Defense League, which exploits the Nazis for its own purposes just as the Nazis exploit Jewish reactions to their uniforms. The JDL and the Nazis thrive on such mutual exploitation.

Given their understanding of the actual impact of American Nazis on public life, leaders of major Jewish organizations could be expected to have little impulse to abandon their traditional commitment to the First Amendment. They know very well that the dangers Jews face from free speech by Nazis are far outweighed by the dangers of suppression of speech. But with constituencies that have learned the lessons of the Holocaust about the need for resistance, and that respond with passion to the Jewish Defense League's slogan if not to its organization, most major Jewish groups are forced to support prior restraint.

As the Skokie case developed and it became plain that it was becoming a great public issue, I met individually with top officers of such important Jewish organizations as the American Jewish Committee, the American Jewish Congress, the Anti-Defamation League, the National Jewish Community Relations Advisory Council, and the Union of American Hebrew Congregations. Not all those groups abandoned their traditional commitment to free speech. But leaders of those that held firm, as well as leaders of those that supported prior restraint, made it plain that constituent pressure was forcing them to limit their advocacy of free speech. This was reported to me, in a few instances, with great embarrassment by people who had been the ACLU's closest allies in many battles for First Amendment freedoms.

The split with the ACLU over free speech in Skokie took on heightened significance for the Jewish organizations because of accidents of timing. It came at the same moment when the United States Supreme Court was considering the *Bakke* case, a challenge to the constitutionality of a program of affirmative action at the University of California designed to increase the number of black and Hispanic students admitted to its medical school. Organizations representing racial minorities and most other "liberal" groups supported affirmative action. Almost all Jewish organizations, on the other hand, opposed the University of California plan. On this issue, leaders of Jewish organizations acted out of conviction rather than merely in deference to constituent pressure.

The Skokie matter also coincided with the Sadat peace initiative and with growing public disenchantment with Israel in the United States because of the Begin government's policies in the period prior to the peace agreement at Camp David. Leaders of Jewish organizations felt constrained not to engage in public criticism. The limits they imposed on themselves, however, damaged their relationships with many Americans sympathetic to Israel's interests who believe Israel should give ground for the sake of peace.

Skokie, *Bakke*, and Begin, in combination, drove apart Jewish groups and their traditional allies. The prospect of isolation—very dangerous to Jews—would be more imminent were it not for another accident of timing. A television "docu-drama" on the Holocaust was broadcast in April 1978, just at the time when the Nazis were expected to march in Skokie. The march was postponed because of developments in the litigation on its right to take place. Publicity about the Nazi plan to march, however, greatly strengthened the impact of the television series. The confrontation between American Nazis in the streets and concentration-camp survivors in Skokie brought up to date and on to home soil a drama about great events that took place in foreign lands years ago. "The silver lining in these clouds," said Abbot Rosen, Director of the Chicago Anti-Defamation League, referring to the Nazi march, "is the renewed consciousness and sensitivity of people to these things."

It remains to be seen, however, whether interest in the Holocaust will be sustained. The subject is painful and people are eager to forget. There was a wave of interest in the early 1960s because of the Eichmann capture and trial. It ebbed quickly. Will that happen again?

Jews can hardly be expected to create alliances with the other segment of the American public that has been most vehement in opposing free speech for the Nazis: left-wing political groups. On the subject of Israel, these groups are the greatest enemies of the Jews. They are the champions in the United States of the Palestine Liberation Organization. Israel, in their view, is engaged in imperialist adventures. Some of these groups are even apologists for the mistreatment of the Jews in Soviet Russia.

Allies are important to Jews. While the Jews are the best organized minority in the United States and, therefore, now exert substantial political influence, they remain extremely vulnerable. They are a tiny minority, making up less than 3 percent of the American population. They are disproportionately concentrated in a few cities that suffer from anti-urban prejudice and in a few marginal industries that can function only in those cities. They are the only minority considered by the rest of the country to be distinctive in both race and religion. And they have close ties to another country that is locked into conflict with nations on which the United States may become economically dependent.

Jewish vulnerability is not a problem for Jews alone. History demonstrates that anti-Jewish prejudice spills over and victimizes others. The Spanish Inquisition burned Christian dissidents along with Jews at the stake. Gypsies, Poles, and other "inferior" people also died in the Nazi concentration camps. So did mental defectives and homosexuals. The Nazi organizations in the United States are as violently anti-black as they are anti-Jewish. For reasons of self-interest if for nothing else, it is urgent that the traditional allies of the Jews remain allies. It should be possible to differ over Skokie, *Bakke*, and Begin while sharing the concern for Jewish survival uppermost in the minds of Jews. The difference should be over the means and not the end.

3

A Symbolic Assault

Frank Collin is fond of saying that he singled out Skokie for his demonstrations "because it's a Jew suburb." In a way, Skokie singled itself out.

In early 1977, Collin wrote letters to about a dozen Chicago suburbs seeking permits for demonstrations in their parks. His Nazis would demonstrate, he said, for white power. Most of the villages receiving the letters ignored them. The Skokie Park District board of trustees, however, wrote back to the Nazi leader that he would have to post $350,000 in insurance in order to hold a rally in the park. The insurance was required, they said, to pay for any damage to park property.

Frank Collin had encountered similar tactics before. The previous summer, the Chicago Park District had put a stop to demonstrations in Marquette Park by denying permits to any group that could not post $250,000 in insurance, thus effectively shutting out Collin's Nazis and such antagonists as the Martin Luther King, Jr. Coalition. Collin called the American Civil Liberties Union and the ACLU began a lawsuit in his behalf to challenge the insur-

ance requirement as an unconstitutional restriction on freedom of speech and assembly. That lawsuit was still pending
in a federal court when the trustees of the Skokie Park District adopted their own regulation, whose specific target was
Frank Collin and his Nazi band.

Frank Collin had become identified with challenges to
insurance requirements. He was a plaintiff in a lawsuit to
invalidate the Chicago Park District's requirement. He could
hardly pass up the opportunity to respond to the Skokie
Park District trustees. He dispatched another letter to Skokie.
The letter reached the village police on March 20, 1977.
Collin announced a demonstration in front of the Skokie
Village Hall at 3 P.M., Sunday, May 1. It would last about
half an hour. Thirty to fifty demonstrators would march back
and forth on the sidewalk, single file. They would obey all
laws and they would not obstruct traffic. In protest against
the insurance requirement of the Skokie Park District, the
Nazis would carry signs with such slogans as "White Free
Speech," "Free Speech for White Americans," and "Free
Speech for the White Man." Collin also took care to inform
Skokie officials that the demonstrators would make no de-
rogatory statements, either orally or in writing, directed at
any ethnic or religious group. They would, however, march
in uniforms. The Nazi uniforms include a swastika emblem
on the armband.

Before Collin's announcement, Skokie's principal claim
to fame was that it was the "World's Largest Village." Those
words were emblazoned on the covers of local booster publications and formed the title for a 1964 magazine article
about Skokie. Forrest Emerson, a one-time Skokie resident,
wrote in *Omnibus* magazine that, "With an expanding population of some 68,000, Skokie is by declaration, fanfare,
ruffles and flourishes—the world's largest village. Beyond
question this is far better than being just another small
city."

The news accounts about Skokie's confrontation with

Collin's Nazis regularly refer to the "Village" of Skokie. And the site where the Nazis sought to demonstrate—in front of the village hall—helps ensure that Skokie is widely perceived as a village. But if a village calls to mind a picture of a cluster of houses, a few shops, and white-steepled churches around a greensward square, that is not Skokie. With a population now between 70,000 and 80,000, Skokie has a municipal budget of more than $30 million a year. There are more than a thousand business establishments in Skokie and the "village" has an industrial gross product of well over $2 billion a year.

Skokie is also a middle-class bedroom community—median family income $22,500—for commuters to Chicago. It reflects Chicago's character as the nation's most rigidly segregated city. Although the average Skokie home sells for between $60,000 and $70,000, these figures do not lie beyond the reach of many blacks. Yet Skokie is virtually all-white.

Ironically, in the years before World War II, Skokie was almost entirely non-Jewish. From the 1830s on, most of the settlers in Skokie, then known as Niles Centre, were Germans and for a century German was a first, and then a second, language. The village acquired the name of Skokie in 1940. When World War II broke out, Skokie was still known as "Little Germany." The German American Bund was still active there and pro-Nazi sentiment was strong.

The two decades following World War II were a period of great growth for Skokie. Some of America's largest corporations established factories, research laboratories, and offices there. "The booming Skokie Valley communities of today," said a special issue of *Skokie Life* published in March 1965 to celebrate industrial development, "are a far cry from the sleepy truck-farming villages that dotted the area not so many years ago." In what was surely hyperbole but suggests how far from a village Skokie has come, *Skokie Life* went on to assert that "today the Skokie Valley ranks as one of the nation's most highly industrialized areas."

Its growth did not do much for the appearance of Skokie's business districts. "Throughout the downtown area," said a 1971 report by the Skokie Planning Commission, "there is not a hint of architectural style or design cohesiveness. The buildings fail to relate to the community, to each other, or even to themselves. In short, there is almost nothing about the physical environment of downtown Skokie which is conducive to ease of traffic movement, auto or pedestrian, or aesthetically pleasing to anyone walking or driving through the area."

The village hall—also known as the municipal building—is a red brick structure erected in 1927. The arrangement of the windows gives it a vaguely Georgian aspect. The building is topped by a small gold dome and weathervane and in front it has white Corinthian columns. A large parking lot adjoins the village hall. On the other side is a short row of businesses—a dry cleaning establishment, a travel agency, a loan company, and a bank. Across the street are a chiropractor's office, a gas station, and a church. Two other churches are within sight, along with a very pleasant and well-stocked library that displayed a fine exhibit of Japanese art when I visited. The sidewalks in front of the village hall where the Nazis asked to hold their march can be seen from the windows of a nearby apartment house.

The post-World War II migration to Skokie included a large number of Jews. Many of them had been residents of the inner-city neighborhoods of Chicago who moved away when the blacks moved in. Skokie was easily accessible to Chicago and not very expensive, a fine refuge. The residential neighborhoods of Skokie, away from the village hall and the nondescript buildings that surround it in the downtown area, are modest and pleasant. The first Jewish religious service took place in 1952, celebrated in the village hall because there was no synagogue in Skokie. A quarter of a century later, when Frank Collin's Nazis informed Skokie of their intention to march, there were nine synagogues.

Fred Richter is a resident of Skokie and president of the Synagogue Council of the Northwest Suburbs, representing 10,000 of Skokie's Jews. When he heard of Collin's plan he acted immediately, convening a meeting of the council. At that March 24 gathering, the council decided to ask village officials for more information, as Richter said later, to be sure that "elements of the organized Jewish community" would not be "acting on its own."

Albert J. Smith, the mayor of Skokie and a Roman Catholic, and Harvey Schwartz, the village attorney, working with the synagogue council, sought to permit the demonstration with as little fuss as possible. They enlisted rabbis in seven Skokie synagogues. At meetings in the synagogues, the rabbis called on their congregations to remain calm and deny the Nazis what they were seeking: attention.

The strategy of constraint failed. The synagogue meetings did not produce calm. Ignoring or "quarantining" the Nazis seemed like poor advice to a survivor of Bergen-Belsen who refused to be "like a sheep again." At every meeting, survivors of the Holocaust stood up to oppose the plan. Their pleas were emotional and irresistible. A mood took hold in Skokie: The Nazis must not march. Never again!

On April 21, Fred Richter and his colleagues met again. This time all the Jewish organizations of Skokie sent representatives, as did Chicago metropolitan and national Jewish organizations. A few people proposed "quarantining" the demonstration. Everybody would stay away and the Nazis would have the sidewalk in front of the village hall to themselves for a half hour on a Sunday afternoon. It gathered little support. A resolution was adopted, instead, to deny the Nazis the right to march, and another resolution called for a counterdemonstration at 11:00 A.M. on May 1 in a parking lot a few blocks from the village hall. Twelve thousand to 15,000 people were expected to participate. Fred Richter said later that the counterdemonstration would remain peaceful as long as the Nazis did not appear but that if the Nazis showed up, it might not be possible to control the counterdemonstrators. And, said Richter, other groups would probably hold counterdemonstrations of their own.

With the demonstration only ten days away, Skokie was at fever pitch. Leaflets appeared in Skokie: "Smash the Nazis"; "No Free Speech for Facists"; "Join us May Day." Apparently, the leaflets were the work of a coalition of left-wing organizations in Chicago that planned to descend on Skokie for their own counterdemonstration. Jewish-surnamed residents of Skokie complained to the police about abusive late-night telephone calls. Although Collin denied that he or his followers had made these calls, the Nazis apparently were responsible for a leaflet that turned up in Skokie: "We carry the swastika," it said, "because it is the ancient symbol of our white people throughout history and the world. It is the sign of total resistance against the niggerization of our country. The swastika is the emblem of racial brotherhood and comradeship among white men everywhere."

Four days before the scheduled march, Skokie began a lawsuit to prevent it. The village attorney, Harvey Schwartz, filed a petition in the Circuit Court of Cook County asking for an injunction to prevent the Nazis from parading in uniform on May 1. When Frank Collin found out about the lawsuit on the afternoon of April 27, once again he called the local office of the American Civil Liberties Union. The call was taken by David Goldberger, legal director of the Illinois ACLU and a Jew, who was already representing Collin in the challenge to the Chicago Park District's insurance requirement. To an attorney like Goldberger, with extensive experience in First Amendment cases, this case seemed clear-cut. He consulted briefly with David Hamlin, executive director of the Illinois ACLU, and Edwin Rothschild, president of the Illinois ACLU. The three were unanimous, Rothschild taking the onus of making the decision. He directed Goldberger to take the case.

For several hours late that afternoon, Goldberger tried to find a volunteer attorney to represent Collin in court the next day. No luck—all were busy with other matters. Goldberger had to do it himself.

Harvey Schwartz's complaint for the Village of Skokie asked for the issuance of an emergency injunction. It recited the facts about Skokie. It is "an Illinois municipal corporation containing a population of approximately 70,000 persons. Included among the population of Skokie are approximately 40,500 persons of Jewish religion or Jewish ancestry or of both Jewish religion and Jewish ancestry. Included among the Jewish population are hundreds of persons who are (a) survivors of Nazi concentration camps and (b) many thousands of persons whose families and close relatives were murdered by the Nazis. A large percentage of the Jewish population is organized into groups and organizations. These groups include the Janusz Korczak Lodge of B'nai B'rith, and others, composed of survivors of the Nazi death camps." The complaint described the National Socialist Party of America and said they "have patterned their conduct, their uniform, their slogans and their tactics along the pattern of the German Nazi Party, including the adoption of the hated swastika." The complaint reported Collin's intention to march in Skokie and the late-night phone calls:

As a result of such phone calls and some publicity given by the news media [Schwartz's legal papers said], it is common knowledge among the Jewish population that the National Socialist Party of America intends to march in the Village of Skokie on May 1, 1977. The threatened march of the defendants [i.e., the Nazis] has aroused the passions of thousands of individuals of Jewish faith or ancestry within the Village and more particularly has aroused the passions of the survivors of the Nazi concentration camps who are taking measures unknown to the plaintiffs [i.e., the Village of Skokie] to thwart the threatened march. The march of the defendants on May 1, 1977, is a deliberate and willful attempt to exacerbate the sensitivities of the Jewish population in Skokie and to incite racial and religious hatred. Said march, if not restrained by Order of this Court, constitutes a grave and serious threat to the peace of the citizens of the Village of Skokie. By reason of the ethnic and religious composition of the Village of Skokie and the circumstances alleged above, the public display of the swastika in connection with the proposed activities of the defendant, National Socialist Party of America, constitutes a symbolic assault against large numbers of the residents of the Plaintiff village and an incitation to violence and retaliation.

Schwartz's court papers established the legal issue that would be debated furiously for a long time to come. He made no allegation that the Nazis would engage in violence. But the display of the swastika, he said, "constitutes a symbolic assault." The only physical violence he anticipated might come from onlookers—those Jews whose passions had been aroused "who are taking measures unknown." The violence to be prevented by a legal prohibition on the march was to be against the marchers, not the counterdemonstrators.

The court convened in the Richard J. Daley Civic Center on the morning of April 28 to consider the Village of Skokie's petition. Circuit Court Judge Joseph Wosik, who must stand for election to his post, presided. Soon after the hearing began, the judge's secretary came into the courtroom to in-

terrupt. Cook County Sheriff Richard Elrod was on the
phone. Judge Wosik left the bench to speak to Elrod, a
Daley machine stalwart whose law-enforcement responsi-
bilities encompassed the Village of Skokie.

"In Cook County," says David Hamlin, the Illinois
ACLU director, during the Skokie controversy, "a cynical
observer would suggest that there was a direct relationship
between the case, the judge, the sheriff's telephone call, and
the outcome of the hearing. A cynic would suggest that all
that remained after the sheriff called the judge was for
Skokie to put on its case."

The first two witnesses for Skokie were Fred Richter,
who testified that a counterdemonstration against a Nazi
march on May 1 might get out of control, and Ronald Lan-
ski, who testified that he had seen the "Smash the Nazis"
leaflets in Skokie. The third witness, Sol Goldstein, a concentration camp survivor and the man whose mother was
buried alive by the Nazis, took the stand. The swastika, he
said, "reminds me [of] my closest family who were sent to
death by the swastika, and it reminds me [of] a threat that I
am not safe with my life. It reminds me that my children are
not safe with their lives." Goldstein also testified, Goldberger's objections about relevancy having been denied, that
he had received phone calls from persons identifying themselves as Nazis. He predicted bloodshed if the Nazis marched.
He did not intend to use violence, but he did not know if
he could control himself when he saw the swastika and
would not promise that he would refrain from attacking
Collin.

"I may," Goldstein said.

Next, Skokie's lawyers called Frank Collin to the stand
as a "hostile" witness. Yes, Collin said, the views of his organization are similar to those of the Nazi party of Germany
and yes, he had read *Mein Kampf* several times and agreed
with much of it. He acknowledged that his organization had
prepared an anti-Semitic, anti-black circular. The Jews, it

said, are responsible for the "black invasion of Southwest Chicago," and, therefore, they would be the targets of "street demonstrations and even speeches" in "Evanston, Skokie, North Shore, Morton Grove, etc."

The fifth and final witness for the village was Albert J. Smith, mayor of Skokie. Conversations with leaders of community and religious groups in Skokie had persuaded him that if the march took place, a violent and uncontrollable situation would develop. No law-enforcement officials testified and no evidence was offered to the court that police would be unable to maintain order.

The evidence on the other side was an affidavit by Collin reciting his plans for a small, orderly, and brief demonstration in front of the village hall on a Sunday afternoon. David Goldberger's hastily prepared legal memorandum seeking dismissal of Skokie's request for an injunction called the request "a classic case in which government officials ask a court of equity to impose a prior restraint on the speech of persons advocating unpopular ideas."

Judge Wosik, unimpressed with Goldberger's legal arguments, proceeded to lecture him on his client's views. "There is no need for me to go on with any impressions of other than this evidence," said the judge. "I think these pamphlets in this situation on these facts are completely repulsive. I think they're intended to cause trouble. I think they are intended to incite riot, to cause bodily harm, and to do all those things that the Constitution does not give a defendant a right to do." He ordered the National Socialist Party of America barred "from engaging in any of the following acts on May 1, 1977, within the Village of Skokie: Marching, walking or parading in the uniform of the National Socialist Party of America; Marching, walking or parading or otherwise displaying the swastika on or off their persons; Distributing pamphlets or displaying any materials which incite or promote hatred against persons of Jewish faith or ancestry or hatred against persons of any faith or

ancestry, race or religion." Goldberger immediately announced the ACLU's intention to appeal the order.

The following afternoon, Friday, April 29, the Illinois
Appellate Court denied Goldberger's motion for a stay of the
injunction against the march. The state supreme court was
not sitting, and that seemed to be the end of the matter for
the weekend. But Frank Collin had other plans. Late that
afternoon he told the press he would march the next day,
Saturday, April 30. The court's order had only specified that
no march could take place on Sunday, May 1. No counterdemonstration was planned, so that rationale for the injunction was not relevant. On Saturday morning, Skokie reached
Circuit Court Judge Harold Sullivan at his home to ask that
Judge Wosik's injunction be modified to ban a march "without limitation as to date or time." Although the Nazis were
not present and had no chance to be heard on the matter,
Sullivan agreed to modify Judge Wosik's injunction and
ordered Collin and company not to demonstrate "within the
Village of Skokie on April 30, 1977 or at any time thereafter
pending further order of this Court."

Collin had already set out for Skokie. His group of six
or seven cars was met by a police car at the Skokie exit on
the expressway. When the police told him about the new
court order, he turned back.

On Monday, May 2, and Tuesday, May 3, Skokie
adopted three new ordinances intended to prevent the Nazis
from marching there. Ordinance 994 purported to "provide
for the safe and orderly movement of traffic." It required
would-be demonstrators on the village streets to get a permit at least thirty days in advance and to post public liabil-
ity insurance of $300,000 and property damage insurance of
$50,000. The device used to keep demonstrators out of parks
was now being used to keep them off the streets. Village
Ordinance 994 also provided that permits would be issued
if the village manager found that "the conduct of the parade,
public assembly, or similar activity will not portray crimi-

nality, depravity or lack of virtue in, or incite violence, hatred, abuse or hostility toward a person or group of persons by reason of reference to religious, racial, ethnic, national or regional affiliation." This ordinance, adopted by unanimous vote of the village trustees, allowed the trustees discretion to waive any of its provisions. Village Ordinance 995 made it a crime to disseminate in Skokie any material "which promotes and incites hatred against persons by reason of their race, national origin, or religion." The ordinance proscribed "markings and clothing of symbolic significance." Village Ordinance 996 nailed down the prohibition on Nazi clothing. "No person," it provided, "shall engage in any march, walk or public demonstration as a member or on behalf of any political party while wearing a military-style uniform." Violation was made a crime. Ordinances 995 and 996 were adopted unanimously.

During May and June, David Goldberger tried in several courts to remove the injunction that banned the march. The Illinois courts were in no hurry to consider the matter, but on June 14 the United States Supreme Court directed the Illinois courts to expedite a decision. Despite that order, the Illinois courts continued to deal with the injunction in a leisurely manner. But Collin grabbed attention again on June 22 by applying for a permit under Skokie's Village Ordinance 994 to hold a march on July 4 in front of the village hall. He could not obtain the $350,000 in insurance, Collin told Skokie, requesting that the village waive the requirement or help him to find an insurer. John Matzer, the village manager, turned him down.

The rejection of Collin's application produced more litigation: an ACLU lawsuit in federal court to invalidate the three ordinances. While that suit was in preparation, yet another court case was brought. The Chicago office of the Anti-Defamation League, acting on behalf of Sol Goldstein and other survivors of the Holocaust, asked that Collin be permanently barred from marching in Skokie, lest he inflict "menticide," a form of emotional harm, on the survivors. It was a novel theory for a lawsuit.

The lawyer for the survivors in the "menticide" suit was Jerome Torshen, an attorney who had provided legal representation to the Daley organization. On June 29, he appeared in court before Circuit Court Judge Archibald Carey, a black with a strong civil rights background. "Evidence in this case," Torshen told Carey, was "as obscene and horrendous as any ever presented in this city." Despite the extraordinary and unprecedented "menticide" claim, Carey denied Goldberger's motions to dismiss Torshen's suit. While it never became a serious part of the legal battle and Torshen never got a chance to present his "obscene and horrendous" evidence, the suit helped to inflame the emotions of all the participants. Torshen's legal papers referred to David Goldberger as "Neo-Nazi Counsel." Goldberger and Hamlin called me in distress about the epithet. Only after I called national officers of the Anti-Defamation League myself in fury and in outrage and got them to call their Chicago counterparts did Torshen back away a bit. He informed the court that this had just been his way of saying "Counsel for the Neo-Nazis."

Several of the actors in this unfolding drama were playing parts outside the courtroom as well, adding heat to the controversy. Frank Collin announced that Nazi "storm troopers" from California, Missouri, New Jersey, Nebraska, Ohio, and Texas would turn up to augment his march in Skokie. Rabbi Meir Kahane, founder of the Jewish Defense League, spoke at a meeting of 350 people on the evening of June 29 at Congregation B'nai Emunah in Skokie and vowed that "if I see a Nazi marching, I will break his head." The standing-room-only crowd in the synagogue was told that "we spit in the graves of 6 million Jews if we allow the Nazis to march." A week earlier, Kahane and about twenty followers had sat in for several hours in the ACLU's national office in New York, disrupting the work of our office. Their demonstration had verged on violence and one JDL member spat on me. They left the offices as soon as they were satisfied that no other reporters they had invited were coming to the event. Later they held similar sit-ins in several other ACLU offices around the country.

Responsible community leaders in Skokie were also devoting increased attention to the march. One of those who decided that the Nazis could not be ignored was Rabbi Laurence Montrose of the Skokie Central Traditional Synagogue. On the lawn in front of the synagogue there are large signs calling attention to the plight of Jews in the Soviet Union. In the vestibule, there is a *Yad Vashem* memorial to the 6 million Jews slaughtered by the Nazis. Rabbi Montrose is regarded in Skokie as the unofficial chaplain to the survivors of the death camps. A quiet man with no taste for violent confrontations, the rabbi wrote to the 640 families in his congregation telling them that it was their "solemn duty" to take part in the counterdemonstration if the court should allow it to go forward. Rabbi Montrose had in mind a peaceful demonstration. Other Skokie residents had different ideas.

Frank Collin and the Nazis did not show up in Skokie on July 4, but the Jewish Defense League did. Thirty-one JDL members, most of them from New York and Miami, marched with black helmets in military formation in a parking lot at the Jewish Community Center. Some carried sticks and clubs. About 2,000 people turned up to watch and news photos of the march were published widely. Some who saw the photos may well have thought it was the Nazis who were marching in Skokie.

On July 12, 1977, the Illinois Appellate Court modified the injunction. The Nazi march could take place, the appellate court said, but without display of the swastika:

The swastika is a symbol [which] is inherently likely to provoke violent reaction among those of the Jewish persuasion or ancestry when intentionally brought in close proximity to their homes and places of worship. The swastika is a personal affront to every member of the Jewish faith, in remembering the nearly consummated genocide of their people committed within memory by those who used the swastika as their symbol. This is especially true for the thousands of Skokie residents who personally survived the holocaust of the Third Reich. They remember all too well the brutal destruction of their families and communities by those wearing the swastika. So, too, the tens of thousands of Skokie's Jewish residents must feel gross revulsion for the swastika and would immediately respond to the personally abusive epithets slung their way in the form of the defendants' chosen symbol, the swastika.

In denying the right to display the swastika, the Illinois Appellate Court relied on what is known as the "fighting words" doctrine, established by the United States Supreme Court in a 1942 case, *Chaplinsky* v. *New Hampshire*. Chaplinsky, a Jehovah's Witness, had been distributing the literature of his sect on a busy street in Rochester, New Hampshire, on a Saturday afternoon. He got into an argument with a police officer and said to the officer, "You are a God damned racketeer" and "a damned Fascist and the whole government of Rochester are Fascists or agents of Fascists." The Supreme Court upheld Chaplinsky's conviction for this outburst.

In the intervening thirty-five years, the "fighting words" doctrine had been applied narrowly by the courts. It had not been used as a justification for prior restraint, as a limit on speech in an entire town, or as a limit on the display of a symbol. The purpose of the doctrine was to permit the punishment of a person who, in a one-to-one, face-to-face encounter, says something so personally insulting as to provoke an immediate and unplanned violent response. The "fighting words" doctrine was so remote from the circumstances of Skokie that the village had failed to cite the *Chaplinsky* case in any of the papers it presented to the Illinois Appellate Court. That court, however, had relied on the *Chaplinsky* case in banning the display of the swastika.

The case went from the appellate court to the state's highest court, the Illinois Supreme Court. Arguments were presented in September 1977 and then a waiting process began. All this time, Collin and his band remained in the news. Newspaper editorial writers and columnists chose sides. Press accounts began to appear on the impact of the case on the ACLU's membership and finances. Much of the debate focused not on whether the Nazis had a right to speak but on whether the ACLU should be defending that right. We should not defend the enemy. The enemy had no rights.

4

"Freedom for the Thought We Hate"

The Illinois Supreme Court decided the case on January 27, 1978, in a ringing victory for the free speech side. The march could not be prohibited, the court said, nor could the Nazis be prohibited from wearing the swastika emblem on their uniforms. The court went on:

> *The display of the swastika, as offensive to the principles of a free nation or the memories it recalls may be, is symbolic political speech intended to convey to the public the beliefs of those who display it. It does not, in our opinion, fall within the doctrine of "fighting words," and that doctrine cannot be used here to overcome the heavy presumption against the constitutional validity of a prior restraint.*
>
> *Nor can we find that the swastika, while not representing fighting words, is nevertheless so offensive and peace threatening to the public that its display can be enjoined. We do not doubt that the sight of this symbol is abhorrent to the Jewish citizens of Skokie, and that the survivors of the Nazi persecutions, tormented by*

*their recollections, may have strong feelings regarding
its display. Yet it is entirely clear that this factor does
not justify enjoining defendants' [the Nazis'] speech.*

Six of the seven judges on the court concurred in the decision. The lone dissenter did not explain his reasons.

The decision produced a flood of phone calls to ACLU offices from news reporters. When several of them asked me how to get in touch with Frank Collin for statements, I declined to help. While I defended Collin's freedom to speak, I did not propose to act as his press agent, and said so. My Chicago colleague, David Hamlin, said I needn't worry, Collin was stranded somewhere between Chicago and St. Louis in one of the many blizzards that afflicted the Midwest that winter. It seemed a delicious irony to Hamlin that our contemptible client would be unable to cash in on his greatest opportunity yet for television and press interviews.

The Illinois Supreme Court's decision left two court cases still pending, the Chicago Anti-Defamation League's "menticide" lawsuit in the state courts brought by Sol Goldstein and other survivors and the ACLU's lawsuit on behalf of Collin in federal court seeking to invalidate the three Skokie ordinances. The Illinois Supreme Court dismissed the "menticide" case in a few days. And, the following month, Judge Bernard M. Decker of the Federal Court for the Northern District of Illinois handed down a fifty-five-page decision declaring Skokie's three ordinances unconstitutional.

Judge Decker was aided in his consideration of Village Ordinance 994, the insurance requirement, by the decision of another federal court in the same district a few months earlier. That court had ruled in favor of Frank Collin in the case David Goldberger brought to challenge the similar insurance requirements of the Chicago Park District. The record in that case had been admitted into evidence in the Skokie case. It included testimony from a licensed insurance broker that she had tried for four or five months to get such insurance for the Nazis. She had contacted thirteen companies and brokerage firms, among them firms which specialized in unusual and hard-to-place lines of insurance. She had failed. She said she believed it would be impossible to obtain such insurance and her testimony was uncontradicted. Judge Decker ruled the insurance requirements unconstitutional because they "impose a virtually insuperable obstacle to the free exercise of First Amendment rights in the Village of Skokie, which obstacle has not been proven to be justified by the legitimate needs of the Village and which may be disposed of at the uncontrolled and standardless discretion of the Village."

Next, Judge Decker turned to what he called the "racial slur" sections of Village Ordinances 994 and 995. The judge raised, considered, and ultimately rejected all of the arguments made in public debates against allowing the Nazis to disseminate racist views by word or by symbol. His conclusion was that the racial-slur provisions of the ordinances were vague and overbroad and that they unconstitutionally imposed a prior restraint on speech.

Finally, Judge Decker considered Skokie Village Ordinance 996, which provided that marches, walks, or demonstrations on behalf of political parties could not take place in military-style uniforms. The only reasons for this ordinance offered by Skokie, Judge Decker noted, were that the wearing of military-style uniforms was "repugnant" both to the "tradition of civilian control of government" and to the "standards of morality and decency of the Village of Skokie." These justifications, said Judge Decker, are "patently insufficient. . . . The First Amendment embraces the freedom to advocate even that the government ought to be violently overthrown, let alone that it ought not to be controlled by civilians. Thus the banning of a symbol which is repugnant to a 'tradition' which all Americans are free to reject and openly criticize is clearly unconstitutional." As for the allegation that such uniforms violated Skokie's standards of morality and decency, Judge Decker saw this as an attempt to subject political speech to the "community standards" criteria that the Supreme Court had employed in considering sexual materials. This approach, said Judge Decker, was impermissible. The uniforms are a form of political speech. The Supreme Court, he pointed out, had made it clear that political speech need not meet standards of acceptability.

Judge Decker said he was "acutely aware of the very grave dangers posed by public dissemination of doctrines of racial and religious hatred."

In this case, a small group of zealots, openly professing to be followers of Nazism, have succeeded in exacerbating the emotions of a large segment of the citizens of the Village of Skokie who are bitterly opposed to their views and revolted by the prospect of their public appearance.

When feelings and tensions are at their highest peak, it is a temptation to reach for the exception to the rule announced by Mr. Justice Holmes, "If there is any principle of the Constitution that more imperatively calls for attachment than any other it is the principle of free thought—not free thought for those who agree with us but freedom for the thought we hate."

Freedom of thought carries with it the freedom to speak and to publicly assemble to express one's thoughts.

The long list of cases reviewed in this opinion agrees that when a choice must be made, it is better to allow those who preach racial hate to expend their venom in rhetoric rather than to be panicked into embarking on the dangerous course of the government to decide what its citizens must say and hear.

Judge Decker's decision appeared to clear the path for the Nazi march. The injunction against it had already been lifted by the Illinois Supreme Court. Insurance bonds would not be required for a permit. And, with the invalidation of the ordinances against racial slurs and military uniforms, the Nazis could not be lawfully punished for marching so long as they were peaceful and complied with the traffic laws.

Displaying ever-increaing flair for getting public attention, Frank Collin announced that he would march on April 20, Hitler's birthday, a date that meant little to most Americans until Collin's announcement.*

April 20, 1978, however, was a Thursday and Collin soon shifted his plans so that he would march on the nearest weekend day, April 22. The new date had another symbolic significance for many of the residents of Skokie: it was the first day that year of Passover.

Howard Goodman, a Skokie native, now a reporter for the *Oregon Statesman*, described the reactions of his hometown residents. "The town's biggest car dealer," said Goodman, was "telling how he marched with Patton and damned if he'll let the Nazis march." He told of a man who placed an advertisement in the Skokie paper to propose that if the Nazis marched at 11:00 A.M., the village should spread horse manure at 10:00. The man said they could clean it up after the Nazi march. In his own family, and within himself, Goodman found divided views. His mother advised his father to stop donating to the American Civil Liberties Union because of its defense of the Nazis' right to march. His father tried to organize a moderate and reasonable protest demonstration, "but he is only dimly hopeful. There are too many crazies. . . . There is an undercurrent of panic."

At home in Skokie, over dinner with his family, Goodman found himself saying, " 'To hell with the First Amend-

---

* I was much more conscious of the date's significance than other people because it was so close to my own birthday, April 22. My mother had told me that she had been fearful that I would be born on April 20 while the massive celebrations of Hitler's birthday were taking place in the Berlin streets outside the hospital windows. She implied strongly that she had done what she could to delay my birth so that it would not take place on April 20.

ment! We cannot allow Nazism to happen again. Not without protest. If I saw a Nazi walking down Oakton Street, I would not trust myself to restrain from violence.'

"We debated some more. Opposing the Nazis' right to march, I heard myself like Bull Connor opposing Freedom Marchers. Soon I was on the other side. 'The only thing that separates a free society from others is the free flow of ideas. Even hateful ideas. Even ideas that may hurt us.'"

As the date for the Nazi march drew near, the Christian churches of Skokie demonstrated their solidarity with the Jewish community. They assembled 2,500 Christian and Jewish residents of Skokie in a high school auditorium for a prayer service. Black armbands with yellow stars on them were distributed to the crowd. Many Christians—in the town known as Little Germany just a generation ago—wore the armbands as a sign of resistance to Nazism and support for its Jewish victims. A few years earlier, the Skokie human relations commission's annual report celebrated as the year's highlight a Christian church's sign on its outdoor bulletin board at *Rosh Hashanah* wishing its Jewish neighbors a good new year. In the year since the first news of the Nazi march, the churches and synagogues of Skokie had spoken with one voice.

One of the church leaders is the Reverend Thomas W. O'Connor, pastor of St. Peter's United Church of Christ, directly across the street from the village hall. When O'Connor was a seminary student, he had participated in civil rights marches. Now, he asked himself what good could come from allowing the Nazis to march in Skokie. "I can find none," said O'Connor. Together with the ministers of the other Christian churches, O'Connor organized support for Skokie's Jewish community and opposition to the Nazis' plan to march.

With the march apparently imminent, once again, plans for a massive counterdemonstration were discussed in earnest. Governor James Thompson of Illinois said he would participate. Senator Charles Percy, speaking on the United States Senate floor on March 14, 1978, said he was joining in a call for a massive counter-rally. "We must never forget that the First Amendment rights of freedom of speech and assembly are the basic underpinnings of our democratic society," said Percy. But in the same speech he said he had "urged townspeople [of Skokie] to pursue to the fullest extent possible their legal remedies to prohibit this offensive display." He did not attempt to reconcile the commitment to First Amendment rights and the call for a legal prohibition on the Nazi march.

Sol Goldstein announced that at the same time and place as the Nazi march a group of death-camp survivors would demonstrate. Governor Thompson wanted no part of a confrontation with the Nazis, he said. He would participate instead in a large and dignified demonstration some distance away. Jewish Defense League chapters around the country issued statements saying that they would violently disrupt the Nazi march. Anyone who stood in their way would face the consequences, they warned. The American Jewish Congress, which had said it would file a friend of the court brief in the U.S. Supreme Court in opposition to the march if that court agreed to hear the case, began to get phone calls from people asking about charter flights to bring people from around the country to take part in counter-demonstrations in Skokie.

Frank Collin and a St. Louis counterpart, Michael Allen, announced that the National Socialist Party of America would hold a national convention in St. Louis on the weekend of March 11 and 12. It would build on the Skokie publicity. The Nazis had recently opened an office in Gravois Park, a section of south St. Louis that resembles the Marquette Park neighborhood in Chicago. A twelve-block march would bring 150 storm troopers on Saturday, March 11 through the south St. Louis neighborhood, where the Nazis believed they had many sympathizers.

ACLU leaders in St. Louis, meeting with city officials, helped to persuade them to avoid a Skokie-like legal battle. The Jewish Defense League made a last-minute effort to get a federal judge to prohibit it, but the march took place on schedule. Forty-three uniformed Nazis rode along the march route on a flatbed truck, protected from a crowd of about 3,000 spectators by 175 police officers.

Bonnie Pechter, who had replaced Rabbi Meir Kahane as the national director of the Jewish Defense League, was one of the spectators. She said that 103 JDL members were dispersed throughout the crowd. Twenty red-helmeted members of the Black and White Defense Committee, a Chicago group, were there also. Some spectators threw snowballs, stones, and soda bottles as the Nazis shielded themselves with their "white power" placards. Six spectators were arrested, one for arriving on the scene with a loaded rifle in an unlocked case. No one was injured. The Nazis gave up their plans for a rally at the conclusion of the ride. Fearful for their own safety, they agreed to transfer to a police bus and stayed sequestered in a police precinct for several hours while someone went to retrieve their civilian clothes. The Nazis changed out of their uniforms at the police station and left quietly. Plans to reassemble at their office were cancelled. They were afraid of an attack. They did manage to rent a hotel room at an undisclosed location, where a few of the Nazis completed their convention. "We have finished our business," Collin announced. "Where we did it makes no difference."

The St. Louis episode was a setback for Frank Collin. He seemed disappointed by the small number of Nazis who had turned up for a national convention. And although the police had provided them with ample protection, the Nazis had been ignominiously routed in a neighborhood where they expected support. They had looked foolish, not menacing. It didn't bode well for the Skokie march. Frank Collin began telling people he might not march on April 20 or 22 after all. He was spared the need to call off his Skokie demonstration, however, when Judge Decker, in a surprising move, announced that he was issuing a forty-five-day stay of his own decision invalidating the Skokie ordinances. The stay, issued three weeks after the decision, was to allow Skokie time to appeal Decker's ruling to the United States Court of Appeals for the Seventh Circuit. Such stays are not ordinarily issued by courts where the effect is to continue a prior restraint on speech.

The stay kept the invalidated ordinances in effect until early May as Hitler's birthday came and went. An immediate confrontation passed.

The Seventh Circuit Court of Appeals acted quickly and, on May 22, 1978, affirmed Judge Decker's decision that the three Skokie ordinances were unconstitutional. The stay was not continued. Again, all legal obstacles had been cleared, or so it seemed. A new date was set, June 25.

Two state senators, however, decided to continue the legal battle. Howard Carroll and John Nimrod introduced bills in the state legislature with language similar to the Skokie ordinances prohibiting group defamation. Illinois had first enacted such legislation in 1917 and, although upheld by the United States Supreme Court in 1952 in a five to four decision, the law was repealed in 1964. It had almost never been enforced in the forty-seven years it was law in Illinois. Senator Nimrod's variation of the old Illinois group-defamation statute was to add a provision making it a crime to parade with symbols having historic associations with political violence.

The decisions by Judge Decker and the Seventh Circuit Court of Appeals had made it clear that laws such as those proposed by Senators Carroll and Nimrod could not now survive judicial scrutiny. Their enactment in state legislation, however, would prolong the legal batle. If a lawsuit is brought in federal court to challenge the constitutionality of a state law, the state has a right to have its appeal heard by the United States Supreme Court. Even proceeding on an expedited basis, the legal battle would drag on another year or more. While the battle was underway, the Nazis would not be able to demonstrate anywhere in the state.

The new group-defamation laws were quickly adopted by the Illinois State Senate. Before hearings on them could be held in the Illinois Assembly, Frank Collin proposed a deal. If the legislation were dropped and he was permitted to demonstrate in Chicago's Marquette Park, he would cancel his plan to march in Skokie.

From Collin's standpoint, it was a very good deal. He had squeezed out of the Skokie litigation most of the attention it would give him. As the Anti-Defamation League put it, the Nazis "received miles of publicity out of every inch of the route of march." The aborted national convention the Nazis held in St. Louis had informed Collin what was likely to take place if he ever got to march in Skokie. All along, he had been more interested in marching in Marquette Park. Despite a federal court decision against the Chicago Park District's bond requirements, Collin was still being kept out. After the court decision holding a $250,000 requirement unconstitutional, the Chicago Park District had reduced the bond to $60,000. David Goldberger was returning to court to challenge the new restriction and would probably dispose of it quickly. But the new state law would keep Collin from demonstrating anywhere in Illinois for at least another year.

"He is not the kind of person you make a deal with," Senator Carroll said when he heard of Collin's proposal. Senator Nimrod added that he "absolutely will not" make a deal. "We should not let the courts or bargaining determine the course or purpose of legislation," said Nimrod, lumping together judicial interpretations of the Constitution and Frank Collin's proposal for a deal.

With only a little more than two weeks to go until the scheduled march, the Illinois Assembly Judiciary Committee met to consider the Carroll and Nimrod bills on June 6. Representatives of Skokie's survivor community journeyed to Springfield to testify. Rabbi Laurence Montrose urged the adoption of the law so that residents of Skokie would not be forced to "take to the streets in their own defense." Mrs. Erna Gans, president of the B'nai B'rith Janusz Korczak Lodge, said the Nazis "equated silence with weakness, with the silence of the world since 1933" and urged the legislators to speak out by passing the laws just as the residents of Skokie had spoken out by resisting the demonstration.

Joel Sprayregen, a prominent Chicago attorney, appeared to testify on behalf of the new laws as a constitutional expert. Since I was there to testify in opposition, the judiciary committee asked us to come forward together to respond to questions and to debate. Sprayregen had been a staff attorney for the Illinois ACLU in the early 1960s and for several years thereafter a member of its board of directors. He and I had worked together closely fifteen years earlier and I tried —without much success—to detect any signs that Sprayregen was embarrassed to appear in opposition to free speech. It seemed evident that his long-time ACLU affiliation was one reason Sprayregen was chosen to oppose me. Sponsors of the new laws, among them the assemblyman from Skokie who is one of the few Illinois legislators who regularly supports civil liberties, also attempted to suggest that ACLU opinion was divided by pointing out that the Supreme Court's 1952 decision upholding the constitutionality of a group-defamation law had been written by Justice Felix Frankfurter, many years earlier a founder of the ACLU.

When my debate with Sprayregen was done, the committee voted. It was a slow process as each legislator spoke for a few minutes to explain his or her vote. As the voting proceeded, it became evident that something remarkable was taking place. Legislators not previously noted for special dedication to civil liberty were speaking eloquently about freedom and constitutional principle. Watching it reminded me of the televised hearings of the committee's congressional counterpart when that body considered the impeachment of Richard Nixon. Discussions in legislative committees are rarely conducted on a high plane, but when it happens it is wonderfully restorative of faith in the democratic process.

The committee voted fifteen to five against Nimrod's bill and sixteen to four against Carroll's bill. Skokie was running out of ways to block the march and, at the same time, Frank Collin was running out of enthusiasm for marching. In Collin's case, it seemed clear that if he marched, he would have few followers. His men were "cowards," Collin said publicly, and he threatened them with $100 fines if they didn't show up for the march. At the same time, Collin repeated that if he could march in Marquette Park, "there would be no purpose in going to Skokie." The Community Relations Service, a "conflict resolution" agency in the United States Department of Justice, searched for ways to allow Collin his Marquette Park march in exchange for calling off the march in Skokie.

Skokie appealed to the United States Supreme Court to reverse the decisions by the United States Court of Appeals for the Seventh Circuit and Judge Decker. Conceding by this time that its ordinance requiring $350,000 in insurance was unconstitutional, Skokie rested its case on the claim that racial slurs expressed either directly or by symbols and military-style uniforms could be prohibited. Skokie also asked the United States Supreme Court for a stay so that no march could take place pending the high court's consideration of the case. On June 12, the Supreme Court denied the request by a seven-to-two vote. Neither the dissenters—Justices Blackmun and Rehnquist—nor the majority explained their votes. On June 13, the Illinois Assembly defeated efforts to override the actions of its judiciary committee and bring to the floor the bills passed by the State Senate to ban the Nazi demonstration. The votes were overwhelming, 110 to 56 against the Carroll bill and 85 to 61 against the Nimrod bill.

Every legal obstacle to the march had been cleared. Only the Nazis themselves could cancel the march on June 25.

Sol Goldstein, who had emerged during the year as the principal spokesman for Skokie's survivor community, announced plans for the counterdemonstration. A few Skokie leaders would gather across the street from the Nazis and recite the names of the death camps and *Kaddish*, the Jewish prayer for the dead. The main body of counterdemonstrators would assemble at a school athletic field about five blocks away. Goldstein said he expected about 50,000 people to take part. State and local police maintaining order would have the assistance of some 200 marshals organized by the public affairs committee of the Jewish United Fund, the official sponsor of the counterdemonstration. They would keep order, Goldstein said, because "to be violent would be to dishonor the memory of those who died. . . . We cannot sink to the level of those we oppose." Sol Goldstein had come a long way since he told a court fifteen months earlier that he did not know whether he could restrain himself from responding violently to a Nazi demonstration.

On June 20, with only five days to go until the Skokie march, a hearing was held in federal court on the Chicago Park District's $60,000 bond. Judge George N. Leighton, who had earlier struck down the $250,000 requirement, announced that he would deal with the reduced bond as an "emergency matter." After hearing arguments by David Goldberger and an attorney for the Chicago Park District, Leighton said, "We could go on for a long time with hearings on this matter but we know from experience in this case that the plaintiff's argument will prevail." Leighton ruled from the bench that the Nazis could march in Marquette Park without posting a bond.

Frank Collin had his out. He canceled the Skokie march and said he would march in Marquette Park on July 9. Collins also said he would go forward with yet another demonstration—this one on Saturday, June 24, at the Federal

Building Plaza in Chicago. Since it was federal government property, local officials had no power to interfere with that demonstration.

The Jewish United Fund called off the counterdemonstration in Skokie. Most residents of Skokie shared with Frank Collin and his Nazis a sense of relief that they would be spared a confrontation. Jewish Defense League leaders, however, expressed disappointment. They were spoiling for a fight. Since there was to be no battle in Skokie on Sunday, they shifted their attention to the Federal Building Plaza rally on Saturday.

The Nazis were scheduled to show up at the Federal Building Plaza at 4:30 Saturday afternoon. When the time came for the demonstration, no Nazis were to be seen but several thousand counterdemonstrators were on hand. Among the organized groups there were forty or fifty members of the Jewish Athletic League from Brooklyn, New York, who had flown in for the occasion, a similar number of red-helmeted members of the Black and White Defense Committee, members of the Revolutionary Socialist League, and, of course, members of the JDL. Rabbi Meir Kahane was in the Chicago area because he had planned to fight the Nazis in Skokie. Kahane did not show up at the Federal Building Plaza, however, because it was the Sabbath.

Prior to the demonstration, Collin had met with Chicago police and federal officials to arrange an escape route through buildings and tunnels. To avoid a clash with the counterdemonstrators, the police escorted Collin and his followers through the escape route in reverse to the site of the demonstration. The Nazis arrived—about a score of them all told—an hour and a half late. Almost all the counterdemonstrators had remained to wait for them. The Nazis were greeted with a barrage of eggs, beer cans, and rocks. They stood their ground for ten or fifteen minutes and then left the same way they came. The police arrested some fifteen of the counterdemonstrators and one police officer was slightly injured by a flying rock. Otherwise, no damage was done. The following day in Skokie several hundred people attended a memorial service for the victims of the Holocaust. In front of the village hall where the Nazis had planned to demonstrate, all was peaceful.

5

"Poisonous Evenhandedness"

The Fight for Free Speech was the title of the American Civil Liberties Union's first annual report. The report reviewed the organization's activities during the year of its founding, 1920, and concluded with a statement of position. "We stand on the general principle," the ACLU asserted, "that all thought on matters of public concern should be freely expressed without interference."

Fifty-seven years later, in 1977, when the Nazis announced their intention to march in Skokie, the stand was the same. "There should be no control whatever in advance over what any person may say," the ACLU contended in 1920. "The right to meet and speak freely without permit should be unquestioned.

"There should be no prosecutions for the mere expression of opinion on matters of public concern, however radical, however violent. The expression of all opinions, however radical, should be tolerated. The fullest freedom of speech should be encouraged by setting aside special places in streets or parks and in the use of public buildings, free of charge, for public meetings of any sort."

The 1920 statement had gone on to deal with public assemblies. "Meetings in public places, parades and processions," the ACLU said, "should be freely permitted, the only reasonable regulation being the advance notification to the police of the time and place. No discretion should be given the police to prohibit parades or processions, but merely to alter routes in accordance with the imperative demands of traffic in crowded cities. There should be no laws or regulations prohibiting the display of red flags or other political emblems."

The ACLU statement of principle was issued in a far more turbulent period than the 1970s. Labor-organizing efforts in the post-World War I period were often punctuated by beatings and shootings. IWW (Wobbly) members were lynched in many western towns. The Russian revolution inspired a red scare. Anarchists exploded bombs in many public buildings and sent a large number of bombs through the mails addressed to judges and other public officials. The home of Attorney General A. Mitchell Palmer was wrecked in one of the bomb explosions as were the homes of several other officials active in World War I sedition prosecutions. Palmer responded by organizing the infamous raids linked to his name by history. Thousands of aliens and suspected radicals were rounded up and jailed without hearings. Several hundred were also deported. And the Ku Klux Klan emerged again with all the strength that it achieved in the Reconstruction years following the Civil War.

Unlike its predecessor of the late 1860s, the Klan of the early 1920s operated nationwide. The "invisible empire" had an estimated 100,000 members in 1921 and by 1924, at peak strength, it dominated elections in many states in the South, the Midwest, and even in the Far West.

The Klan, according to the ACLU reports of the period, was one of the primary threats to freedom of speech. Its armed night riders regularly disrupted meetings of their opponents. Yet even then, when the ACLU was devoting much of its energy to efforts to secure prosecutions of Klansmen for violent interference with the rights of others, it defended free speech for the Klan itself. The ACLU's second annual report, *A Year's Fight for Free Speech*, in 1921 described the organization's efforts to protect the rights of Klan members. "The New York City police," said the report, "break up meetings of the Ku Klux Klan and . . . handle Klan activities in the same lawless manner as they often handle radicals." The ACLU had come to the aid of the Klan. "Although we are, of course, uncompromisingly opposed to the principles and activities of the Klan," the ACLU asserted, "nevertheless we have demanded for them as for everyone else the free exercise of their civil rights without official interference."

The ACLU maintained its policy of defending the freedom of all to speak throughout the 1920s and the 1930s although in the dark days before the United States entered World War II the policy came under heavy fire. The war had been underway for a year in Europe and it seemed likely that the United States would be drawn into it. Yet the ACLU was still insisting that American Nazis and Fascists had a right to speak. When the Hitler-Stalin nonaggression pact was signed, it also seemed possible that the United States would find itself at war with Soviet Russia. It was in the face of these events that the ACLU issued a leaflet in October, 1940, *Why We Defend Civil Liberty Even for Nazis, Fascists and Communists*.

"The American Civil Liberties Union," the leaflet reported, "is subject to increasing criticism for continuing to defend the civil rights of Nazis, Fascists and Communists.

" 'How can you,' these critics ask, 'defend the civil liberties of movements which, if they achieved power, would destroy civil liberties? Have not events abroad revealed the danger of these movements? Should we not sacrifice their liberties to save our democracy in a crisis where national unity is imperative? Can we allow propaganda in behalf of foreign dictatorships to endanger our own democracy?' "

The "critics" did more than raise questions. Some were ACLU members who resigned when Arthur Garfield Hays, the ACLU's general counsel, went into court to defend free speech for a Nazi or for a Communist. But the 1940 leaflet insisted that the organization would not waver in the face of such defections: "The defense of democracy demands the maintenance of freedom of speech, press, assembly and the right to the ballot for all minorities, whatever their character or purposes. Once the liberties of unpopular minorities are sacrified, no liberties are safe. The heart of democracy is civil liberty for everybody without distinction."

Despite the leaflet's brave words, however, the ACLU succumbed to some of the pressures of 1940 and, after a bitter internal dispute, adopted a resolution (known thereafter as the "1940 resolution") barring from its governing personnel members of "political organizations supporting totalitarian dictatorships in any country." While the resolution included by name such organizations as the German American Bund and the Silver Shirts, its real target was membership in the Communist Party. Soon after the resolution was adopted, the ACLU board implemented it by expelling one of its number, Elizabeth Gurley Flynn, a Communist Party leader.

The 1940 resolution and the expulsion of Flynn were hotly debated in the ACLU at the time and ever since. Supporters of the resolution contended that its adoption by an organization that defended the rights of Nazis, Fascists, and Communists exemplified Voltaire's famous statement, "I detest what you say, but I will defend to the death your right to say it." Opponents regarded the 1940 resolution and the Flynn expulsion as betrayals of principle. The ACLU itself, they said, was penalizing people for their associations. The 1940 resolution was rescinded in 1967 and some years later the expulsion of Flynn was posthumously rescinded.

The adoption of the 1940 resolution had its principal

impact during the 1950s. Because the resolution had established the ACLU as anti-Communist, Communists and their sympathizers did not flock to the ACLU for assistance when their civil liberties came under attack in the McCarthy period. A number of organizations emerged with the special purpose of defending the civil liberties of left-wingers. And some ACLU officials who had fought battles against Communists within their own organization were slow to defend the civil liberties of Communists under attack by the government. Most of the state affiliates of the ACLU were vigorous in their defense of the civil liberties of Communists during the 1950s, but a few employees of the ACLU national office were more preoccupied with keeping their own organization free from any possible Communist taint. The lengths to which national ACLU officials went in the 1950s in protecting the ACLU against Communist influence only became publicly known during the summer of 1977. At that time, the ACLU obtained from the FBI the files the Bureau had maintained on the ACLU from its beginnings in 1920. The FBI files, which the ACLU imediately made public, disclosed that the ACLU's Washington office director during the 1950s, Irving Ferman, regularly informed the FBI about persons active in state affiliates of the ACLU who Ferman thought were espousing left-wing causes. The impact of that discovery is still resounding.

As the 1950s ended and the national ACLU acquired new leadership, the organization reverted to its historic role of defending forcefully the civil liberties of everyone, no matter what their political persuasion. During the 1960s, the ACLU court cases dismantled virtually all of the loyalty tests that had been established by government agencies during the previous decade's red scare. Many of the clients in these cases were Communists who had sought help elsewhere when they had legal difficulties during the 1950s.

In 1943, the federal government had prosecuted thirty

American Nazis and Nazi sympathizers under the Smith Act. The ACLU had opposed the passage of the 1940 Smith Act, which made it a crime to *advocate* overthrow of the government by force. The ACLU also condemned the prosecution of a group of Trotskyists under the Smith Act in 1941, a prosecution that had been endorsed at the time by the Communist Party. When the Nazis were indicted under the Smith Act, the United States had been at war with Nazi Germany for more than a year. Despite wartime pressures, the ACLU denounced the prosecution of the Nazis, but did not provide legal representation to them because the Nazis facing prosecution appeared to be enemy agents who had gone beyond the exercise of First Amendment rights and had committed overt acts helpful to Germany. The ACLU's protest, therefore, was limited to attacking use of the Smith Act and conspiracy charges against the Nazis because such charges punished the Nazis for speech.

The ACLU faced the question of defending free speech for a self-proclaimed Nazi for the first time in more than a decade and a half when George Lincoln Rockwell appeared on the scene in the late 1950s.

In the intervening years after the war, the ACLU had defended free speech for such rabid bigots as Gerald L. K. Smith and Father Terminiello. But a Nazi, at a time when the full horror of Nazism was known, was different. The cases Rockwell brought to the ACLU in 1960, however, seemed clear-cut and the organization readily agreed to provide him with legal representation.

The ACLU membership had grown rapidly by this time. In 1950, when Roger Baldwin retired after thirty years as the ACLU's executive director, the organization had 9,000 members. Baldwin had not been very interested in the size of the ACLU's membership; in his efforts to build the ACLU's strength, his main concern had been to attract an elite to the organization, people who could speak influentially on behalf of civil liberties. Baldwin's successor, Patrick

Murphy Malin, launched a membership drive. As a result, the organization had grown to about 45,000 members at the end of the 1950s.

In 1960, the New York Civil Liberties Union filed suit in Rockwell's behalf challenging New York City's refusal to allow the American Nazi Party to hold a meeting in Union Square Park. A former member of the NYCLU Board of Directors, Newbold Morris, Commissioner of Parks of the City of New York, was the principal defendant in the lawsuit. Thus, the ACLU was suing a friend on behalf of an enemy. "The unpopularity of [the Nazi's] views, their shocking quality, their obnoxiousness, and even their alarming impact is not enough," said an appellate court in ruling in favor of the Civil Liberties Union and upholding Rockwell's right to speak. "Otherwise the preacher of any strange doctrine could be stopped; the anti-racist himself could be suppressed, if he undertakes to speak in 'restricted' areas."

The case of *Rockwell* v. *Morris* became an important precedent for the protection of the free speech of dissident groups. But in 1960, like the Skokie case of 1977–1978, it aroused great controversy. New York, ACLU critics pointed out, was home for more Jews and more refugees from Hitler's death camps than any other city in the world. A Nazi march in New York would be even more horrible than anyplace else. Many persons who had joined the ACLU during the period of great growth in the 1950s when it had no occasion to defend free speech for professed Nazis were shocked by the defense of Rockwell's rights. More than a thousand resigned in protest. Many more members allowed their memberships to lapse in protest. But the impact on the ACLU's finances was not severe. 1960 was a period of great growth for the ACLU. During that year, sit-ins began in the South in protest against racial segregation in public accommodations. In 1961, when *Rockwell* v. *Morris* was decided, the freedom rides were underway. The ACLU's role in organizing legal support for civil rights demonstrators won the organization many new adherents. Their influx more than compensated for the losses suffered over the defense of Rockwell's rights.

Then, too, the defense of free speech for Rockwell was probably responsible for more new members than were lost. During the 1950s, many Americans were fearful of joining any organization that defended the rights of Communists, lest they be labeled as Communists or Communist sympathizers themselves. Despite its lapses during the 1950s, the ACLU defended the rights of Communists often enough to make many people afraid to join as members. By defending free speech for Rockwell, the ACLU demonstrated its own evenhandedness. People who had been previously reluctant to join could derive security from the knowledge that if they were ever questioned about membership they could respond, "Yes, the ACLU defends the rights of Communists. But that is because they defend everybody's rights. They even defend the rights of Nazis."

Throughout the 1960s, Rockwell and other Nazis sought ACLU legal representation. Whenever we agreed that a free-speech issue was at stake, which was often, we defended their rights. Rockwell seemed to travel with a list of ACLU phone numbers in his pocket. Sometimes he would be arrested almost as soon as he set foot in a town. If it was late in the evening, or a weekend, he would use the one phone call he was allowed to make to call the home of an ACLU attorney.

Rockwell attracted few supporters but his appearances always got attention. Lenny Bruce summed up the Rockwell era by defining an American Nazi as "two Nazis and a hundred Jews looking around and wondering why so many Jews were there." But despite the outrage Rockwell's appearances aroused, ACLU affiliates providing legal representation to the Nazis got few letters of resignation from members. After the large number of resignations in 1960, there were never more than a handful at a time. Members who stuck with the ACLU in 1960 or who joined later in the decade were well aware of the organization's insistence on defending free speech for Nazis and, apparently, approved.

Some of the lawyers who defended Rockwell on behalf of the ACLU paid more heavily than the organization itself. One lawyer in New York who had embarked on what looked like a promising political career found himself on a radio talk show one night with Rockwell as a fellow guest. Would he defend in court Rockwell's right to speak? the host asked the attorney, who regularly handled civil liberties cases. Yes, he answered.

The next time Rockwell was arrested in New York City, he called to ask the attorney to make good on that promise. The attorney agreed to defend Rockwell so long as it could be done under the auspices of the Civil Liberties Union. He called me at the New York Civil Liberties Union where I was then the director, and asked me to authorize the case. I did.

The attorney won, but his political career was aborted. He was reviled in neighborhood newspapers and spat upon by shoppers in his neighborhood supermarket. Soon thereafter, he cancelled a plan to run for public office.

During the 1960s we handled more free-speech cases than at any time previously in the ACLU's history. We defended free speech for thousands of civil rights demonstrators in the first half of the decade and for tens of thousands of antiwar demonstrators in the second half of the decade. ACLU membership grew from 45,000 in 1960 to 140,000 in 1970.

After Rockwell's death in 1967, American Nazis often had difficulty exercising their right to speak and the ACLU regularly defended their rights, but the cases passed with little notice. Nazis were no longer as much of a novelty as in the early days of Rockwell. They lacked a recognizable leader. Then too, the streets were so crowded with demonstrations of all sorts in the late 1960s and early 1970s that the appearance of a few Nazis attracted little interest.

Many people joined the ACLU to combat Richard Nixon's efforts to suppress civil liberties. Protests over the war in Vietnam, "law and order," Nixon, impeachment, women's rights, abortion, the backlash against desegregation, political surveillance, and FBI and CIA abuses all drew outraged support. In 1974, the year of Nixon's resignation, ACLU membership reached its highest point ever, 275,000. All this time, we were defending free speech for Nazis.

The country cooled down. Demonstrations became infrequent as many protest movements declined and some disbanded. But the Nazis persisted. With little competition in the streets, they became more visible. Even before Skokie, Nazi demonstrations in several other cities attracted more attention than at any time since the early days of Rockwell.

In 1977, many ACLU members, most of them new members in that decade, were shocked to discover that their organization defended free speech for Nazis. In turn, ACLU leaders were shocked that the members hadn't known the ACLU's policies all along.

I was one of those who was most astounded by the reaction of ACLU members to the Skokie case. It took me a long time to realize why a significant number of members had misunderstood the ACLU's policies. The fault, it became clear, was in our (my) failure to provide adequate information to the membership. It was not enough, Skokie proved, to say that the ACLU defends everyone's right to speak.

In the course of a visit to Columbus, Ohio in early 1978, I had an opportunity to gauge the different reactions that would be elicited by stating a principle abstractly and by applying it to a hard case. I was interviewed about the Skokie case on QUBE, a pioneer cable television station equipped for two-way communication between it and its viewers. By pressing a button, viewers can register an instant reaction to anything broadcast on the station.

During the interview, a film sequence was shown of a Klan demonstration on the steps of the state capitol building in Columbus. When viewers were asked whether such groups should be permitted to hold demonstrations, 52 percent signaled yes, 48 percent said no. I followed this immediately by asking the viewing audience whether everyone should be allowed to demonstrate. This time, 80 percent of the viewers said yes, only 20 percent said no. I had simply rephrased the question. Most of those who had said just moments before that they would deny the Klan the right to speak found it irresistible to say yes when asked whether everyone should have that right.

More than 4,000 ACLU members responded to the publicity about the Skokie case by sending in angry letters of resignation. Some returned their membership cards, probably not noticing that the First Amendment is printed on it. Others sent in postcards, oblivious to the fact that the stamps said, "The Right of the People Peaceably to Assemble."

Several times the number who wrote letters of resignation silently allowed their memberships to lapse. All told, the case probably cost the ACLU about 30,000 members—15 percent of its membership—and about $500,000 a year.

Proportionately, there were no more resignations than at the time *Rockwell* v. *Morris* was filed in 1960. But the Skokie case had a very different impact on the ACLU's finances. The Rockwell case came at a moment when there was a great upsurge in ACLU membership. Also, in helping to overcome 1950s fears about joining organizations that defended the rights of Communists, the *Rockwell* case may even have helped the ACLU in recruiting new members. Things were different in 1977. ACLU membership had already declined from the high point of the electrifying impeachment fight of 1974 and, even without the Skokie case, would have declined further. Nothing melodramatic was happening in the country to attract significant new membership to the ACLU.

Only a handful of people joined the ACLU in 1977 *because* of the Skokie case. Those few seemed to regard Skokie as proof that the ACLU was not just another liberal organization but meant what it said about defending everyone's rights.

The Skokie case did not prove divisive in the ACLU's leadership. The Illinois ACLU board of directors was unanimous in its decision to go forward with the case and the board of directors of the national ACLU was unanimous in endorsing the actions of the Illinois ACLU. Not a single one of the thousands of membership resignations came from a person who served in a leadership position in the ACLU.

The united ACLU response to Skokie was in sharp contrast to Ku Klux Klan free-speech cases at Camp Pendleton, California and in Mississippi. On November 13, 1976, thirteen or fourteen black marines armed with knives, clubs, and screwdrivers raided a barracks room at Camp Pendleton where they thought members of the Knights of the Ku Klux Klan, David Duke's organization, had gathered. Five of the seven white marines in the room at the time had to be hospitalized for injuries they suffered during the assault.

There had been growing strife between whites and blacks at Pendleton, a huge marine base that sprawls over many miles of the California coastline north of San Diego. A Klan organization had been formed a few months earlier at Camp Pendleton; buttons, posters, and stickers with racist slogans were widely displayed on the base. White marines and black marines openly carried bowie knives. There had been several minor incidents of violence between individual whites and blacks.

Although the door to the room the black marines raided was adorned with "white power" stickers, the black marines made a mistake. A Klan meeting was in progress, but in a nearby room. The white marines who were the victims of the assault were not associated with the Klan. They apparently were doing nothing more than holding a beer party.

The United States Marine Corps took action against both the white marines who belonged to the Klan and the black marines accused of taking part in the assault. Fourteen black marines were arrested on felony charges. If convicted they faced long prison sentences. Searches were conducted of lockers thought to belong to Klan members. In one of the lockers, the Marine Corps discovered what appeared to be a Klan membership list. Those marines whose names appeared on it were transferred to other Marine Corps installations around the country to separate them both from Camp Pendleton and from each other.

Members of the Klan immediately contacted the San Diego chapter of the ACLU, chartered by the Southern California affiliate of the ACLU. The chapter referred the case to one of its most active volunteers, Michael Pancer, who had won an NAACP "Freedom Fighter" award for his defense of black servicemen in another military case. Pancer filed a lawsuit in federal court challenging the power of the Marine Corps to transfer the whites to other bases because of their Klan membership and seeking damages for those marines punitively transferred in violation of their First Amendment rights of association.

The lawsuit provoked a dispute in the parent Southern California ACLU. Reports circulated that the Klan members had been transferred not merely because of their membership in the Klan but because they carried bowie knives, which they called "nigger stickers," and because they had stockpiled weapons. At a turbulent meeting of the board of directors of the Southern California ACLU in early December 1976, a motion was adopted with a one-vote margin (twenty-six to twenty-five) to ask the San Diego chapter to drop the lawsuit. The San Diego ACLU did not budge.

At the request of the Southern California ACLU, I visited Camp Pendleton in December 1976. I wanted to investigate the event and to recommend a course of action which might prove acceptable both to the San Diego chapter and to its parent group, the Southern California ACLU. Major General Carl Hoffman, the commander of Camp Pendleton, who had ordered the transfers, made it plain to me that the possession of weapons by Klan members played no part in his decision. Bowie knives were commonplace at Camp Pendleton, he said. And while the searches of the lockers of suspected Klan members had turned up a .357 Magnum, General Hoffman thought this was a minor matter. Such guns were available for purchase at stores on the base. Although an infraction had been committed in the failure to register the gun, no disciplinary action had been taken against the gun's owner for not registering it because it was not considered serious. General Hoffman said he had transferred those persons believed to be Klan members solely because they were Klan members, in the hope of defusing racial tension.

I discovered that the Marine Corps had also violated the civil liberties of the black marines facing criminal charges as a result of the assault the previous month. Charged with conspiracy to assault as well as with assault, black marines would be implicated if they had participated in conversations before the assault. The conspiracy charge made them all responsible for each other's acts.

The raid was over in a few moments and witnesses made only two identifications. It was easier to identify those black marines who had participated in militant conversations and charge them with conspiracy. And by roping in additional defendants, the conspiracy charge enlarged the number of blacks with whom plea bargains could be negotiated in exchange for statements incriminating others.

After arrest, the black marines had to wait periods of at least seventy-two hours before they saw defense counsel. During those days and nights, they were interrogated. With the help of promises that things would go easier for them if they confessed, some incriminating statements were obtained. By the time I visited the brig where they were confined, the black marines had been locked up for a month, yet no showing had been made that they were likely to evade trial. Pretrial confinement in the military does not automatically result in the reduction of time that must be served as punishment for any crime proven at trial.

I recommended that the ACLU attempt to protect the civil liberties of both the Klan members and the black marines. The Southern California ACLU agreed with that recommendation. It furnished legal representation to the black marines facing criminal charges and, in a reversal, also endorsed the lawsuit by Michael Pancer on behalf of the Klan members punitively transferred.

"Organized verbal and non-verbal conduct on a military base of a racist nature (e.g., anti-black, anti-Jewish and the like)," Bayard Berman, an attorney on the board of directors of the Southern California ACLU, had written to his fellow board members when they considered the Camp Pendleton case, "is simply not protectible free speech and is subject to reasonable regulation by the military authorities." Berman's view had been supported by another attorney on the board, Martha Goldin, who wrote, "The transfer of the Klansmen was not simply an attack upon their rights of speech and association. The KKK members at the base were not racists by organizational reputation alone; they were self-avowed racists. They did not presumably believe in white supremacy; they posted virulent literature which proclaimed their position. They did not only use speech to express their views; they acted upon them." The seven black members of the Southern California ACLU board, who asked that the San Diego chapter be directed to withdraw from the lawsuit, had also written to their fellow board members, "The complaint refers to symbolic free speech, such as the wearing of white power patches and the display of white power slogans, isolating those manifestations of Klanism from the context in which they were provocatively exhibited. . . . Behind this cloud of free speech purism, pitched battle was being waged by black and white protagonists."

Such comments, while commonplace elsewhere, are very strange coming from members of the board of an ACLU affiliate. "Organized verbal conduct" and the display of "virulent literature" are what the ACLU regularly defends against suppression. And while derisive comments about "free speech purism" are frequently made by antagonists of the ACLU, its "pure" position is a source of pride within the ACLU. Those members of the Southern California ACLU board who opposed representation of the Klan pointed out that there was evidence that Klan members went beyond speech and engaged in overt acts such as the collection of weapons. But the ACLU's traditional role is to insist that if acts are alleged that violate proper laws and regulations, they must be proven. Any punishment must be solely for those acts. Punishment must not be based on the political views, however obnoxious, of those charged with unlawful acts. At Camp Pendleton, the Marine Corps had punished Klan members because they were Klan members. No attempt was made to prove that any of the Klan members had engaged in unlawful acts.*

* I was not enthusiastic about the lawsuit on behalf of the Klan members at Camp Pendleton, even though I thought it was right in principle. I told leaders of the Southern California ACLU that I thought it was highly unlikely that a court would interfere with the power of the Marine Corps to punish servicemen—or to "defuse" the situation at Camp Pendleton, as the base commander put it—by transferring them to other bases. The courts, I thought, would be very reluctant to suggest that any member of the armed services had a right to remain at a particular base. Even if a decision to transfer marines were based on mere whim, and not just on an understandable desire to avoid trouble, it would be sustained by the courts.

Once the suit on behalf of the Klan members had been brought by the San Diego chapter, however, there seemed to be no alternative but to support it publicly. Predictably, the lawsuit did not succeed in interfering with the discretionary power of the Marine Corps to transfer servicemen.

The reasons why an opposing view demonstrated some strength bear examination. The Southern California ACLU is one of the largest and strongest affiliates of the ACLU. It defines the term "civil liberties" far more broadly than other parts of the organization. Inadequate health care and economic policies that foster unemployment are civil liberties issues to the majority of the Southern California affiliate, though not to most of the rest of the ACLU, who want the organization to limit its focus to issues of traditional civil liberties concern.

Many of the Southern California ACLU board members are politically radical. Almost instinctively, many members of that board would align themselves with organizations which express "solidarity" with black marines at Camp Pendleton who complain about Klan-generated racism on the base. Racism is prevalent at Camp Pendleton. It overstates the influence of the Klan, however, to suggest that it played a major role in generating the racism. The emergence of a Klan unit at Camp Pendleton was more of a symptom than a cause. Still, the black marines at the base had well-founded reasons for complaining about racism. With such solid ground for rallying to the aid of the black marines at Camp Pendleton, some members of the board of the Southern California ACLU were appalled that their organization should also be providing legal assistance to the enemies of the black marines, the Klan. They perceived a direct conflict between legal aid to the black marines and legal aid to the Klan members.

Those who believed that the ACLU should provide representation to both groups also worried about the appearance of such a conflict, but the argument prevailed for representing both Klan members and blacks because both had the same legal antagonist in court: the U.S. Marine Corps. The Marine Corps had violated the civil liberties of both groups with a certain impartiality.

"Do not defend the enemy" was the argument of another organization that rallied to the aid of the black marines at Camp Pendleton, the National Lawyers Guild. The Guild, an organization of about 5,000 lawyers, law students, and others, founded in 1937, uses the word *progressive* most often to describe its own politics. It is progressives—not the enemy—who deserve defense. The Guild has been successful in keeping within its membership "old left" lawyers with loyalties to the Soviet Union and the Communist Party of the U.S.A., "new left" lawyers who are members of an "Anti-Imperialist Caucus" that opposes the policies of the Soviet Union and the CPUSA as much as it opposes the foreign policy of the American government, and several other varieties of left-wingers. Some of the young lawyers active in the Guild are only vaguely radical and have no sectarian ties.

The National Lawyers Guild was active in the 1960s and the early 1970s in providing legal assistance to civil rights demonstrators, to antiwar demonstrators, and to draft resisters. It often worked side by side with the ACLU. Some lawyers active in one were also active in the other. But while the ACLU defended the rights of right-wingers as well as left-wingers and most of its court cases could not be politically labeled, the Guild was exclusively concerned with defense of the rights of members of "progressive" movements.

Representation of the Klan by the San Diego chapter of the ACLU provoked the Guild to do something it had carefully avoided throughout the period in which Guild lawyers and ACLU lawyers had worked together. The Guild denounced the ACLU in a statement entitled "Sterile Civil Libertarianism Builds Racism." The statement was issued in March 1977 on behalf of the National Lawyers Guild by its president, William Goodman, a Detroit lawyer. "When the ACLU fights for Klan members against being transferred because of their Klan activities," the Guild asserted, "it must argue that the Klan has a right to organize, speak out, grow, and develop at a military base like Camp Pendleton. . . .

When their lives and freedom are threatened in this way, black people can be expected inevitably to fight back. They should not only be expected to fight back in a militant and forceful way, they should also be vigorously supported in that fight." The implication was that the Guild endorsed the violent response by black marines to the emergence of the Klan at Camp Pendleton.

As for the ACLU, the National Lawyers Guild said it was guilty "of a poisonous evenhandedness." The statement went on:

To say that progressive people such as anti-war activists, communists, anarchists, and anti-imperialists, are to be treated in the same way and accorded the same defense by the ACLU as is accorded to Nazis, Fascists (such as the Reverend Moon) and to the Klan, will ultimately weaken support for civil liberties amongst progressive and militant people in struggles in this country. Support for one side, the progressive side, should be wholehearted and provided in the spirit of comradeship. Support for the other side, the reactionary side, may be appropriate at times. On a specific and limited civil liberties issue, it may be correct for the ACLU and other forces to lend some legal support by way of amicus participation. However, support should be miserly and stingy—limited to the most proscribed of circumstances and focused upon the narrowest of issues.

William Goodman sent the statement to members of the Guild who were also active in the ACLU "in the hopes," as he put it in a covering memorandum, "that somehow the issue can be raised nationally." The issue was not "raised nationally" right away but it became a factor several months later.

The dispute over the representation of the Klan at Camp

Pendleton was not confined to the Southern California ACLU and it did not end with their decision to endorse the lawsuit. It attracted a great deal of public attention, very little of which focused on facts of the case. The major issue for the public seemed to be whether the ACLU should defend the rights of groups such as the Klan. This astonished me because the ACLU was already representing Klan members in other cases at the time of the Pendleton incident just as it had represented Nazis, Klan members, and their ilk throughout the ACLU's history. The Skokie case was not yet underway and I had no inkling of the controversy it would produce.

The ACLU had started one of its Klan cases about a year before the Camp Pendleton episode. Charles Holland, a corrections officer at Walkill prison in New York State who had been a member of the Independent Northern Klan (no connection to David Duke's organization), was threatened with discharge, although he said he had resigned from the Klan, if he did not sign a statement pledging neither to associate nor correspond with any known Klan member, to avoid any meetings of the Klan or meetings where Klan members were present, and to refrain from distributing any Klan literature. He refused to sign and the New York Civil Liberties Union brought a lawsuit in his behalf challenging the power of the state corrections department to require him to do so.

New York State Corrections Department officials asserted that they had good reason to take action against prison guards who are active in the Ku Klux Klan. Because most prison inmates in New York are members of racial minorities and because guards—most of whom are white—exercise power over the lives of the prisoners, racism could lead to violent outbursts. The memory of the riot at Attica prison was fresh in the minds of officials of the department.

While these concerns cannot be dismissed lightly, they did not fit Charles Holland's case. In thirty-three years as a guard, he had never filed a complaint against a prisoner and no prisoner had ever filed a complaint against him. At the time the corrections department began looking into his Klan activity, he had been employed for several months as an "arsenal officer," a post he had sought and intended to hold until retirement. As arsenal officer, Holland reported to work at midnight and was locked in the arsenal, alone, to guard its contents. The arsenal was unlocked at 8:00 A.M. and he went home. He had no contact with prisoners.

After receiving the New York Civil Liberties Union's legal pleadings reciting these circumstances, the New York State Corrections Department dropped its effort to discharge Charles Holland. But the Holland case was used by opponents of the ACLU's defense of Klan members at Camp Pendleton as further evidence of our insensitivity to the rights of Klan victims. That was the way William Kunstler characterized it in a debate I had with him about Camp Pendleton before a law school audience. Kunstler apparently knew nothing of Holland's record or of the duties that kept him away from prisoners until I had a chance to respond during the debate.

Another case created a dispute within the ACLU. In Houston, a Nazi group had sponsored a recorded telephone message that told listeners, "We are beginning a battle by offering a $5,000 prize for every non-white killed during an attack on a white person." It called for race war "against Jews and other non-whites." A Houston television personality, Marvin Zindler, brought a lawsuit to prohibit the taped message from being played. A state court ordered that the message be dropped and, the next day, Southwestern Bell Telephone Company disconnected the number.

The matter came before the board of the Houston ACLU in early December 1977. The Nazis had asked us to defend them on the grounds that their First Amendment rights had been violated. As the board met, I joined the discussion by telephone from New York and urged the chapter not to provide direct legal representation. Was this inconsistent? I had urged the opposite course in all the other Nazi and Klan cases during the year. But the Houston case seemed different. I told the members of the chapter board that an offer of money to commit an act seemed to me to be an overt act not subject to the constitutional protection accorded to speech. I suggested as an analogy that free speech would protect any effort to persuade legislators to vote a particular way but if money were offered to any legislator to vote that way, it would be considered an attempt at bribery. Free speech would not cover the offer of a bribe. Nor would it cover an offer of payment for killing someone. Nevertheless, I urged the chapter to enter as a friend of the court (*amicus curiae*). The court order against the recorded message was overly broad. It not only prohibited the offer of money, but it also prohibited advocacy of race war, and that was speech. The chapter could make the distinction if it entered as *amicus* rather than directly, for if it entered directly it would have to defend against the court order in its entirety.

The Houston ACLU board voted eleven to five neither to represent the Nazis directly nor to participate in the case as a friend of the court. Three attorneys active in the chapter immediately announced that they would represent the Nazis individually because they believed the entire message should be subject to free speech protections. One of the attorneys, Michael Maness, also announced that he was resigning as a member of the chapter board because of its failure to defend the Nazis' free speech.

With the aid of the attorneys who dissented from the decision of the Houston ACLU, the Nazis quickly won their legal battle. The case was decided on procedural grounds. A Texas appellate court ruled that the Nazi messages were "disgusting and repugnant" but that Marvin Zindler lacked standing. He had failed to demonstrate to the court how he would personally be harmed by the recorded message.

But it was a Klan case in Mississippi, not Nazis in Skokie, that proved to be by far the most divisive within the contemporary ACLU. While about 97 percent to 98 percent of the ACLU's membership nationwide is white, the small Mississippi ACLU prided itself on its biracial composition. About a third of its members are black and, at the beginning of 1977, a third of the members of its board were black. Then, at the beginning of August 1977, Douglas Coen, Grand Dragon of the Gulf Coast Knights of the Ku Klux Klan of Saucier, Mississippi, wrote a letter to the Harrison County Board of Education asking for the use of the Saucier school ball park for a rally on a Saturday, August 13, 1977. It would be a "peaceful rally," said Coen, "open to the public regardless of race, creed or religion. . . . The Sheriff's Department and the Mississippi Highway Patrol will be notified of the event and will be welcome, in an official or unofficial capacity."

The Saucier school ball park had been used for meetings by many other groups and the time of year and the day of the week selected for the rally ensured that it would not interfere with any school programs. School was out for the summer. The rally would be open to all, regardless of race or religion. The Harrison County Board of Education, nevertheless, turned down the Klan's request to use the ball park.

The Klan appealed to the Mississippi ACLU for legal representation. A volunteer attorney, Robert Labine, and Grand Dragon Coen appeared before the next weekly meeting of the Harrison County Board of Education to ask it to reconsider its decision. Nothing doing. The rally, said the board of education, "would not be conducive to the best interests of the school system."

Labine's appearance on behalf of the Klan at the school board hearing ignited a dispute in the Mississippi ACLU.

The dispute over Camp Pendleton and the shock waves from Skokie reverberated in Mississippi. The day after news stories appeared describing Labine's representation of the Klan, a member of the Mississippi ACLU board, Martha Bergmark, sent a memorandum of protest to the members of the group's executive committee. "I believe that the very existence of organizations like the Klan and the Nazi Party poses an actual clear and present danger to the physical safety and civil rights of minority people," said Bergmark. "The issue of defending the so-called free speech rights of fascist gangs, whose very purpose is to deprive minority people of free speech and other constitutional rights, could scarcely provide more graphic proof that many constitutional rights do not exist in a vacuum but that in many cases the rights of one group must be weighed against the conflicting rights of others." Several other members of the Mississippi ACLU board wrote letters objecting to representation of the Klan. A board meeting was quickly convened to deal with the issue.

Astonished and disturbed by the reaction of board members, Mary Ramberg, the Mississippi ACLU director, called the national ACLU seeking assistance. I decided it would be best if a member of the national board of directors from the South represented the national ACLU at the Mississippi meeting. On short notice in late August, it was difficult to reach anyone to go. But one of those called, Clinton Deveaux, was available and instantly agreed to go to Mississippi.

Deveaux is a young black attorney who was then the president of the Georgia ACLU and represented Georgia on the national ACLU board of directors. The meeting he attended in Mississippi was marked by heated debate. Deveaux found himself regarded by the blacks in the Mississippi ACLU as an outside agitator who, coming from Georgia, couldn't be expected to understand the problems of Mississippi. The upshot was a seven-seven vote on representation of the Klan. Richard Johnson, the chairman of the Mississippi ACLU, cast a tie-breaking vote in favor of a lawsuit in behalf of the Klan.

The matter did not end there. Continuing turmoil over the filing of the lawsuit required the Mississippi ACLU board to hold another meeting on the case a couple of weeks later. Mary Ramberg telephoned me and asked me to attend. I did and urged, as Deveaux had at the previous meeting, that the ACLU had to defend everyone's freedom to speak. Labine's lawsuit on behalf of the Klan had been filed by this time and his court papers became an issue in the dispute. The Klan organization he represented, the papers said, "does not advocate the overthrow of the United States Government, nor is Petitioner [the Klan] in any manner subversive or promote violence as a means to effectuate political change." Whether or not this particular Klan organization promoted violence, Klan organizations generally had a long record of violence. One of the white members of the Mississippi ACLU board who opposed taking the case, Edward King, still bore on his face the scars of beatings he had endured during the civil rights struggles of the early 1960s. A member of the family of one of the black members of the board had been a victim of a Klan lynching many years earlier.

A head-on confrontation was avoided at the meeting I attended. Instead, the Mississippi ACLU board adopted resolutions calling for new procedures for taking cases and calling for an educational program directed against Klan activities. About ten days later, the seven black members of the Mississippi ACLU board released a public statement: "We do not and will not succumb to the pressure of the National ACLU representatives that have come here to sell us on the acceptance of the Klan as a client." The seven resigned from the board. They were joined by three whites. Only eleven members were left.

Several persons, black and white, were elected to the

board to fill the vacancies. When procedural difficulties with the lawsuit on behalf of the Klan required it to be refiled in federal court, the Mississippi ACLU board decided to treat the refiling as if it were a new lawsuit and, in a reversal, declined to authorize the case. ACLU procedures provided that the national organization could override a state affiliate's decision on a case only by a vote of the national executive committee. I presented the matter to the ACLU executive committee in January 1978 and, by a divided vote, that body authorized the filing of the ACLU lawsuit in federal court on behalf of the Klan. Because overriding a state affiliate was considered a serious matter, however, the executive committee decided to treat its decision as a recommendation to the full national board of directors.

The national board of the ACLU considered the matter in early March 1978, in a debate marked by rancor on both sides. Had the national office interfered with a local affiliate's prerogatives? Some argued that it had. Had the national office threatened excommunication? The charge was made and denied. Would the Klan rally have a bad impact on black children attending the Saucier school which, like many other schools in Mississippi, is under a court order to desegregate? Did children's rights take precedence over the First Amendment or were the two consistent with each other? Did the nature of the Klan preclude defense of its free speech rights? Several members of the board, convinced that the national ACLU should enter the case only as a friend of the court, argued that direct representation might require the ACLU to lend its name to representations such as those Labine had made when he said in his state court papers that the Klan organization he represented did not promote violence.

There was never any real question what stand would be adopted by the national ACLU board despite the often heated debate. The free speech issues were clearer here than at Camp Pendleton. The issue seemed remarkably similar to Skokie—defending the enemy. The only remaining question was the one identified by the National Lawyers Guild. If the ACLU were to lend support, would it be "by way of amicus participation . . . miserly and stingy?" Or would it be wholehearted, in the same manner that the Guild said that the ACLU should defend free speech for "anti-war activists, communists, anarchists, and anti-imperialists?" Should the enemy be defended directly or not?

Edward King, Mississippi's representative on the national ACLU board, had proposed an *amicus curiae* role in the Klan case to the board of the Mississippi ACLU. As *amicus*, the ACLU would not directly represent the Klan, it would only file a brief with the court on the civil liberties issues at stake. The ACLU ordinarily enters a case as *amicus* when the client has other counsel and the ACLU nevertheless wants to intervene, or when a civil liberties issue is but one element in a case and there are other issues the ACLU does not want to address. An example in the latter category is a murder case in which there is a question as to the admissibility into evidence of a coerced confession. The ACLU might say in an *amicus* brief that the confession is inadmissible but would express no opinion on whether the person charged with the murder committed the crime. The Mississippi Klan case fit neither criterion. The Klan had asked the ACLU for direct legal representation. And the free speech issue was not one of many, it was the only issue in the case.

When the proposal to the Mississippi ACLU for *amicus* participation in the Klan case got no support, the idea was dropped. Edward King became the most outspoken opponent of representing the Klan. The *amicus* proposal was taken up within the national ACLU board by Frank Askin, a Rutgers University law professor. Askin wrote a memo to the ACLU board in early 1978 identifying another ground for filing an *amicus* brief. The ACLU limits itself to *amicus* participation when direct representation might require attorneys defending the client to take anti-civil liberties positions. An example is a case in which defense of a client would make it necessary to compel a journalist to disclose confidential sources. To avoid conflicts between an attorney's duties to a client and ACLU policies, *amicus* participation is appropriate.

"Among the allegations which will likely be raised against the Klan's suit for use of the school field," Frank Askin wrote to the ACLU board, "will be a claim that the proposed rally is merely one overt act in a conspiracy on the part of the Klan to intimidate black and white citizens of the community from cooperating in the legal efforts to desegregate the school." An ACLU lawyer representing the Klan directly "would thus be placed in a position of publicly supporting the Klan's role in the school desegregation controversy and denying that the Klan is engaged in a conspiracy to intimidate anyone or to block the enforcement of a desegregation program."

This argument for *amicus* participation proved far more palatable within the ACLU board than the National Lawyers Guild's proposal that the ACLU defend free speech for the left wholeheartedly and for the right in a miserly and stingy manner. Ultimately, however, it came to the same thing. After the 1950s, when the ACLU was often "miserly and stingy" in defending the civil liberties of the far left, we had never been deterred from defending freedom of speech for Communists by allegations that a "rally is merely one overt act in a conspiracy." Such allegations were made regularly by those who wanted to deny Communists the right to speak. Or Nazis the right to speak in Skokie. The ACLU had not denied the existence of a Communist conspiracy and it need not deny the existence of a Klan conspiracy, any more than it had denied the malevolent intent of Nazis. The ACLU would assert that such allegations are no basis for denying the freedom to speak. A rally cannot be an "overt act in a conspiracy."

In the ACLU board's forty-seven–fifteen vote to provide direct representation to the Klan in Mississippi, Askin himself voted with the board's majority in favor of direct representation, persuaded in the course of debate that ACLU lawyers representing the clients directly would fulfill their duties to their clients and, at the same time, would not have to espouse anti-civil liberties positions.

Several opponents of direct representation of the Klan asserted that the case was not analogous to Skokie. Yet the distinctions are difficult to see. The Nazis are at least as offensive as the Klan, though the Klan may be more dangerous in the United States because it has more adherents than the Nazi organizations. The Skokie demonstration was planned for a public street and the Mississippi demonstration for public property regularly used for political rallies. The Klan demonstration would probably frighten many black residents of Saucier but no more than the Nazis would frighten concentration camp survivors in Skokie. Both were cases of prior restraint.

Then, too, the dispute in the Mississippi ACLU and in the national board of the ACLU over a Klan case followed the dispute in the Southern California ACLU over a Klan case. During the year, the ACLU had defended free speech for Nazis in Detroit, Florissant, Missouri, Milwaukee, San Jose, St. Louis, and Skokie. The only dispute over a Nazi case took place in Houston, where even the strongest free speech advocates in the ACLU believed that an offer of money to commit an act went beyond speech. Nazis cases that were analogous to Mississippi and Camp Pendleton never proved divisive in the board of an ACLU affiliate or in the national board of the ACLU.

The best explanation I can provide is that a National Lawyers Guild-like partisanship for defense of the rights of "progressive" people has some adherents in the ACLU. They are a minority in the ACLU, but strong enough in a few affiliates and on the national board to force divisions on

Klan cases such as Camp Pendleton and Mississippi. Black servicemen at a marine base and black residents of a town in Mississippi are "progressive" people to this wing of the ACLU. In its zeal to protect "progressive" people, it finds reasons not to defend free speech for their enemies. The death camp survivors in Skokie are victims of the most horrible oppression in human history, but they are not "progressive" people whose causes are regularly espoused by groups such as the National Lawyers Guild. Protecting them against free speech was never an issue for the wing of the ACLU that resisted defense of free speech for the Klan.

Accidents of geography also played a part. The Skokie case was the responsibility of the Illinois ACLU, an affiliate with a strong commitment to the evenhanded application of civil liberties principles. Camp Pendleton lies in the territory of the ACLU affiliate where partisanship for "progressive" causes is strongest. Even in Southern California, however, most members of the affiliate board endorsed the actions of the San Diego chapter in representing the Klan once it became clear that mere membership in the Klan was the basis for punitive transfer by the Marine Corps.

The Southern California ACLU's discomfiture over representing the Klan at Camp Pendleton was evident in a suit it filed a few months later *against* the KKK. David Duke had attracted nationwide attention by announcing that his Klan organization intended to patrol the Mexican border to "stem the rising tide of color washing over our border." According to Duke, 1,000 Klansmen, aided by infrared scopes, CB radios, guns, and KKK-marked cars would guard the border from California to Texas.

It was a pipe dream. The Klan had no capacity to organize a paramilitary operation even remotely approaching that magnitude. It was not clear that anything was being done by the Klan beyond its attention-getting announcement. But the Southern California ACLU filed suit against

Duke, the California coordinator of the Klan, Thomas Metzger, and the Klan itself. The suit was filed under a federal law adopted in 1871 as an anti-Klan measure making it unlawful for private persons to conspire to deprive others of their rights.

Most of the ACLU's work is intended to protect citizens' rights against the government. The ACLU rarely files lawsuits such as the case brought in Southern California, but all those I can recall charged the government with failing to enforce the law against private persons interfering with the rights of others. When I was director of the New York ACLU in the 1960s, we filed such a lawsuit against construction workers who had beaten up antiwar demonstrators. The defendants included New York City police who failed to protect antiwar demonstrators. Similarly, the national ACLU filed a lawsuit in 1978 against people who vandalized an abortion clinic and disrupted operations. The defendants included public officials who refused to enforce the law against opponents of abortion.

The Southern California ACLU suit against the KKK made no allegation that public officials had failed to enforce the law against Klan violence. Such an allegation was not a legal prerequisite, but without it the case was out of character for the ACLU. As the director of another ACLU affiliate wrote to me at the time, "I assume that the machinery of the law is still working in Southern California and that the suit against the KKK serves no purpose except public relations." When the suit came before U.S. Judge Howard Turrentine, he declined to issue even a temporary restraining order against the Klan, noting that the KKK had not yet injured anyone or committed any crime.

Another factor in the split in the Mississippi affiliate was the board's pride in its biracial composition. Some whites thought it was more important to keep the blacks on the board than to be evenhanded in defending civil liberties. My own view is that the ACLU needs blacks and whites who will defend free speech for all. To expect less wholehearted commitment to civil liberties from blacks strikes me as patronizing. Black attorneys have appeared in court on behalf of the ACLU to defend the rights of white racists just as Jewish attorneys have defended the rights of anti-Semites. And while the Klan may be especially terrifying in Mississippi, Nazis are especially terrifying in Skokie. In every material way, the two cases are analogous.

The debate over the Mississippi Klan case at the March 1978 meeting of the ACLU board of directors produced its clearest ideological division in many years. The vote demonstrated that those committed to evenhanded defense of civil liberties were in firm control. Had similar debates taken place in the boards of the ACLU's fifty state and regional affiliates and in the boards of its nearly 400 local chapters, with a few exceptions the votes for evenhanded defense of free speech would have been more lopsided. Despite the large number of membership resignations and despite the vocal minority in the ACLU's leadership that shares the National Lawyers Guild's views, the controversy over the Nazi and Klan cases produced greater unity and a surer sense of purpose in the ACLU than at any time in the last decade. It was the only full-scale debate in the national board of the ACLU on any of the current crop of Klan or Nazi free-speech cases. After the national board voted to have the national ACLU represent the Klan directly to secure their right to use the school ball park for a rally, the decision produced no additional disruption in the Mississippi ACLU. Soon thereafter, however, Mary Ramberg submitted her resignation as the affiliate's executive director. Even though her position had won out, Ramberg's differences on the matter with many people in the local organization, when added to the weariness produced by several years of civil liberties struggles in Mississippi, made her decide it was time to quit. In August 1978, a year after the Klan first sought permission to hold a rally in Saucier, Mississippi, the national ACLU's lawsuit challenging exclusion of the Klan came before a Federal court. The judge suggested the school board reconsider its policy. The school board took the hint. The Klan rally was held in Saucier in September 1978 without incident.

The Klan and the Nazis were teamed in one of the free-speech disputes of 1977 when David Duke and Frank Collin appeared together on a half-hour television program recorded in the studios of WHYY, Philadelphia's public television station. It originates just one program that is broadcast nationally on the Public Broadcasting Service network, "Black Perspective on the News." The producer and moderator, a black journalist, Reginald Bryant, invited Duke and Collin to appear on his interview program in September 1977. The program with Duke and Collin included film clips of interviews with black leaders such as the Reverend Jesse Jackson and Mayor Maynard Jackson of Atlanta. Joining Bryant in interviewing the Klansman and the Nazi were two blacks: a Harvard historian, Lawrence Reddick, and an Atlanta psychologist, Charles King.

Announcement of the program stirred an uproar in Philadelphia. A large rally was held on the street in front of WHYY's studios to protest the plan to broadcast. Messages denouncing WHYY were spray-painted on its walls. Several Philadelphia organizations issued statements demanding that the program not be aired. Many donors to WHYY called to say they would never contribute again. Some viewers said they would never again watch the station's programs nor allow their children to see programs it broadcasts, such as "Sesame Street." The day before the broadcast of the Duke and Collin interview, a Jewish community group went to a local court in Philadelphia to seek legal prohibition. The Philadelphia judge asked WHYY President James Karayn to bring the tape of the program to court for an advance screening. That way, the judge said, he could determine whether broadcast of the program would create a clear and present danger of violence. Karayn refused to submit the tape of the program for prior censorship. Very well, said the judge, since he hadn't been able to see the evidence, he would stop the broadcast.

The injuction was issued only a few hours before the scheduled broadcast. It was the first time, as far as anyone could remember, that a court had forbidden the broadcast of a television program. Lawyers for the station, joined by lawyers from the Public Broadcasting Service and from the ACLU, rushed to an appellate court and quickly secured a decision overturning the injunction. The show went on in Philadelphia as scheduled. WHYY followed its broadcast immediately with a thirty-minute discussion in which representatives of Jewish organizations and civil rights groups denounced the program for giving Duke and Collin an opportunity to express their views to large groups of people.

Nationwide, fewer than half of the television stations that ordinarily air "Black Perspective on the News" broadcast that particular program. Some had reasons ostensibly unrelated to the program's content. New York City's Channel 13, a station that did not air the Duke-Collin interview program, was embarrassed when the American Jewish Congress issued a public statement appearing to take credit for keeping it off the air. That forced Channel 13 to come up with a creative solution. Rather than broadcast the offending segment of "Black Perspective on the News," Channel 13 produced its own hour-long program about the dispute. The Channel 13 program included discussion of the dispute by panelists expressing varied views and long excerpts from the program in which Duke and Collin appeared. That way, Channel 13 was able to say to its New York audience that it had not been intimidated.

The refusal of many public television stations to broadcast the Duke-Collin interview raised a difficult question.

Should they be forced to broadcast it? No, I believe. That would interfere with free speech as much as a prohibition on broadcast. Station managers should be free to make editorial decisions. Yet it was clear that the reason some stations declined to air the program had far less to do with editorial decision making than with fear of reprisal by public agencies that provide some of their funds and big private donors.

In the end, the only course that seemed open was to urge stations to carry the program just because it was controversial. That course was not entirely satisfactory. Station managers should not be asked to air programs that have no value beyond their capacity to excite dispute. In this instance, however, public television stations had demonstrated their confidence in the producers of "Black Perspective on the News" by regularly broadcasting the program. By rejecting an episode in which offensive views were expressed, they appeared to be engaged in censorship, not editorial decision making.

Some years ago, a public library board in a small town in Rockland County, New York, adopted a policy asserting that if anybody objected to a book in the library on moral, political, or religious grounds, the librarian should take this as an indication that the book was of more than routine interest and make certain an adequate number of copies were on hand. I wish that spirit had prevailed among managers of public television stations.

In its effort to rebuild its finances after the membership defections, the ACLU proclaimed proudly its own insistence on holding firm on Skokie. Although it was only one of some 6,000 court cases the ACLU took on in a year, Skokie was singled out as the basis for a fund appeal to the entire ACLU membership signed by David Goldberger, the attorney who represented the Nazis in Skokie. The ACLU also enlisted more than 130 other organizations, among them such groups as the American Jewish Committee, the American Jewish

Congress, the NAACP, the Union of American Hebrew Congregations, and the Urban League, as co-sponsors of a National Convocation on Free Speech. The convocation brought together leading figures in government, law, industry, labor, journalism, and the arts to make a public commitment to the support of free-speech principles. It was also a fund-raising event. Its theme, free speech, meant that donors were forcefully reminded of the ACLU's most controversial case as they were asked to write their checks.

6

The Constant Battle

"I accuse," said Emile Zola, France's best-selling novelist, as he indicted the nation's military establishment for framing Captain Alfred Dreyfus, suppressing evidence favorable to Dreyfus, and conducting a "vile campaign" against him.

For a quarter of a century, ever since the economic crash of 1873 after the Franco-Prussian War, anti-Semitic hysteria had been building in France and Germany. A few Jews had been among the speculators who were blamed for the economic crash. The word *anti-Semite* was invented at the end of the 1870s by Wilhelm Marr, a German and one of the leaders of the movement to blame all the ills of society on the Jews. Jews had only recently been labeled as members of a separate race—the Semites—classified as such by a French scholar and professor of Hebrew, Ernest Renan. In the 1880s, anti-Semitic leagues started up in Europe and members attended international anti-Semitic congresses. Edouard Drumont's book, *La France juive devant l'opinion* ("Jewish France in Public Opinion"), attributed to the Jews every trouble in France. The culmination of this anti-Semitic campaign was the accusation that Captain Alfred Dreyfus, a Jew, had betrayed French military secrets.

The accusation and Dreyfus's conviction provided the proof anti-Semites had been seeking of the treason of the Jews. Despite French law, which punished as a crime any libel that defamed people individually or as members of a group, no prosecution for group libel was ever brought against Drumont or any of the other anti-Semites.

Zola's "J'accuse" was published in a newspaper, *l'Aurore*, on a January day in 1898. The next day, the French Assembly adopted a resolution calling for a criminal prosecution. Emile Zola himself was indicted for defaming the military leadership of France. Georges Clemenceau, the "tiger of France," owner of *l'Aurore*, who was to become the nation's premier twenty years later, was also indicted. In a divided jury verdict, they were both convicted; Zola was sentenced to a year in prison, Clemenceau to four months. Although the convictions were overturned on appeal, Zola was tried again later in the year. By then, however, the mood in France was so ugly that Zola went into hiding without waiting for the verdict and escaped to England, where he lived in exile.

Zola had acknowledged the risk of a prosecution for publishing "J'accuse." No anti-Semite was prosecuted, but Zola, who defended a Jew, was convicted. When a government enjoys the power to suppress defamatory statements or to punish those who make them, a Zola is more likely than a Drumont to become the target. The anti-Semitism of a Drumont served the government's interests because it identified convenient scapegoats for economic and military problems and social unrest. Zola's accusations, on the other hand, embarrassed the government. Thus he became, as he well understood, the obvious candidate for a defamation prosecution.

Prosecutions based on speech that embarrasses the government go back in time at least as far as the trial of

Socrates for corrupting the youth of Athens by "making the worse appear the better cause." The issues that arose in Skokie—group defamation, prior restraint, symbolic speech, street demonstrations, hostile audiences, clear and present danger, fighting words, advocacy of illegality—have been the battlegrounds for free speech for centuries.

The United States, its Constitution, and its Bill of Rights are the outgrowth of the long struggle for freedom of speech in England. While the great codifier of the common law, Lord Edward Coke, asserted that there were precedents, the earliest criminal prosecutions for libel in England seem to have been brought in the infamous court of the Star Chamber during the last years of the reign of Queen Elizabeth I. Before that time, libel was only a civil offense. An injured person could recover damages from a person who defamed him individually, but no criminal prosecution could be brought against anyone who defamed a person either as an individual or as a member of a group.

In the court of the Star Chamber in England, criminal prosecutions for libel became synonymous with political repression. In the early part of the seventeenth century in England, a period of great political and religious ferment, the government attempted to suppress public discussion of new doctrines with libel prosecutions. Often, prosecutions were brought against authors who denounced whole classes of people and, therefore, were alleged to have libeled particular individuals who were members of such a class even though nothing had ever been said against the persons individually.

In 1634 a lawyer named William Prynne was tried in the Star Chamber. His crime was that he had published a book that libeled the participants in the plays and dances of the time—one chapter in his book was entitled "Women Actors Notorious Whores." Although the book had been written several years earlier, the timing of its publication proved costly to Prynne. A few weeks before it was published, Queen Henrietta Maria, wife of King Charles I, had taken part in a stage play. Because he libeled women actors as a group as whores, Prynne was charged with calling the queen a whore. He was sentenced to stand in the pillory, to have his ears cut off, to spend the rest of his life in prison, and to pay a large fine. It was an unpopular decision. Outrage at the cruelty of the punishment was an important cause of the English revolution and the execution of King Charles in 1649. Prynne himself, who had been freed from prison, opposed the execution.

To prevent the publication of libels in advance, a system of licensing, or prior restraint, was devised in England. It stayed in effect throughout most of the seventeenth century, leading to John Milton's classic argument for free speech, the *Areopagitica*. Milton's essay of 1644 remains today the most eloquent of all arguments against prior restraint.

By the eighteenth century, the court of the Star Chamber had long since disappeared and the repression associated with it was considered a black mark on the history of England. Licensing had also ended and prior restraint was not tolerated. Even William Blackstone, no paladin of liberty, wrote in the *Commentaries on the Laws of England*, the basis of the American legal system, "The liberty of the press . . . consists in laying no previous restraints upon publications."

Prosecutions for criminal libel persisted nonetheless. In the American colonies, the most famous criminal prosecution for libel was brought against a printer, John Peter Zenger, publisher of a newspaper, the New York *Weekly Journal*, that regularly attacked the policies of the colonial governor. Zenger was arrested for libel in November 1734 and remained in prison until he was brought to trial the following August. He continued to edit the newspaper from his prison cell. At the trial, the judge instructed the jury that its only role was to decide whether Zenger had published the statements that were alleged to be libelous. Since Zenger freely admitted publishing the newspaper, his conviction would have been assured. But at the urging of Zenger's lawyer, Andrew Hamilton, the jury disregarded the judge's advice and freed Zenger. His acquittal became the first great landmark in the history of freedom of speech and the press in America.

The authors of the Declaration of Independence and the United States Constitution were close students of the seventeenth- and eighteenth-century political trials in which battles were fought over freedom of speech, the press, and assembly. There was no great division among them over the protection of these rights, only over how best to accomplish it. The eventual solution was the adoption of a Bill of Rights as a series of amendments to the Constitution, after several states made it plain that they would not ratify the Constitution unless such guarantees of liberty were spelled out and incorporated in it.

The spirit of freedom was at high tide when the Constitution was adopted in 1789 and when the Bill of Rights was ratified in 1791. It ebbed quickly, however, in the wake of the French revolution and terror, the threat of war with France, and the Whiskey Rebellion in Pennsylvania. In 1798, Congress adopted the Sedition Act, punishing by prison and fines the publication of false, scandalous, or malicious writings against the Congress, the president, or the judiciary if the intent was to defame these government officials, or to stir up hatred against them.

The Sedition Act was soon discredited and state legislatures, as in Kentucky, declared it "void, and of no force." Indeed, its unpopularity led to the defeat of the Federalist party. When Jefferson became president, he pardoned all those who had been convicted under the act and Congress eventually repaid all the fines.

Congress again adopted legislation modeled on the

Sedition Act more than a century later, when public support
for liberty was again at low tide. The World War I Espionage Act, amended in May 1918, punished uttering, print-
ing, writing, or publishing any disloyal, profane, scurrilous,
or abusive language, or language intended to cause contempt, scorn, contumely, or disrepute to the form of government of the United States, the Constitution, the flag, or the
uniform of the army or navy. State laws were patterned on
the act. The consequence was the gravest period of political
repression in American history. Rose Pastor Stokes was sentenced to prison for ten years merely for saying, "I am for
the people and the government is for the profiteers." Eugene
V. Debs, the socialist leader, and Victor Berger, a member
of Congress, went to prison for similar remarks. A man in
Minnesota got a prison sentence for saying to volunteer
knitters, "No soldier ever sees these socks." A tailor named
Jacob Abrams was convicted and sentenced to twenty years
in prison for conspiring to publish disloyal, scurrilous, and
abusive language about the government of the United
States.

In the United States Supreme Court, Abrams's conviction was upheld, with Justices Oliver Wendell Holmes, Jr.
and Louis D. Brandeis dissenting. "Persecution for the expression of opinions seems to me perfectly logical," said
Holmes. "If you have no doubt of your premises or your
power and want a certain result with all your heart you
naturally express your wishes in law and sweep away all
opposition. To allow opposition by speech seems to indicate
that you think the speech impotent. . . . But when men
have realized that time has upset many fighting faiths, they
may come to believe even more than they believe the very
foundations of their own conduct that the ultimate goal
desired is better reached by free trade in ideas."

Holmes went on to enunciate the principle that was
attacked so frequently by opponents of permitting the Nazis
the right to march in Skokie:

The best test of truth is the power of the thought to get itself accepted in the competition of the market. . . . That at any rate is the theory of our Constitution. It is an experiment, as all in life is an experiment. Every year if not every day we have to wager our salvation upon some prophecy based upon imperfect knowledge. While that experiment is part of our system, I think that we should be eternally vigilant against attempts to check the expression of opinions we loathe and believe to be fraught with death, unless they so imminently threaten immediate interference with the lawful and pressing purposes of the law that an immediate check is required to save the country. . . . Only the emergency that makes it immediately dangerous to leave the correction of evil counsels to time warrants making any exception to the sweeping command, "Congress shall make no law . . . abridging the freedom of speech."

Most of the Espionage Act continued in effect until 1976. Although what remained of it after the 1918 amendments were repealed in 1921 was supposed to apply only in time of war, we continued living for more than a quarter of a century under a national emergency proclaimed by President Truman in December of 1950 at the time of the Korean War. The remaining provisions of the Espionage Act were sweeping enough to have allowed the Nixon administration to proceed under this law in indicting Daniel Ellsberg in December 1971 for disclosing publicly the contents of the Pentagon Papers.

The repeal of the worst features of the Espionage Act in 1921 and the suspension of the rest of the act because the nation was not at war did not end the free-speech battles of the 1920s. It was a decade of great controversy over symbolic speech. By 1921, thirty-three states had adopted laws making it a crime to display the red flag at any public

assembly or parade if the purpose was to promote any political, economic, or social principle or doctrine. Some states
banned the wearing of red neckties or buttons as symbols of
political viewpoints. Kansas said that the display of any
emblem was forbidden if it was "distinctive of bolshevism,
anarchism or radical socialism." In state legislative testimony
that echoed in Skokie more than half a century later, a New
York City police official said that the red flag had to be
prohibited because it would enrage spectators and the spectators would become violent. "It has the effect," said In-
spector Thomas J. Tunney, "of creating a feeling on the
part of Americans that they would like to assassinate everybody carrying the red flag; or at least a large number of
them feel that way." All during the 1920s, state courts upheld the constitutionality of "red flag" laws on such grounds.
In 1931, a red-flag case reached the United States Supreme
Court, no sympathetic forum for advocates of free speech in
the 1920s, but more responsive now with Charles Evans
Hughes, successor to William Howard Taft, as Chief Justice
of the United States.

Yetta Stromberg was a California teenager who directed
a Communist-affiliated summer camp for children. Every
morning, the children assembled at the flagpole to watch the
red flag run up and they recited the workers' pledge: 'I
pledge allegiance to the workers' red flag and to the cause
for which it stands, one aim throughout our lives, freedom
for the working class." Yetta Stromberg was convicted under
California's red-flag law and sentenced to serve five years
in prison. With Hughes writing the majority opinion, the
Supreme Court decided by a seven-to-two vote that she
should go free and that the red-flag law was unconstitutional. Justices Brandeis and Holmes, who still served on the
Supreme Court, enjoyed the rare experience of siding with
the majority in a free-speech case.

The Hughes Supreme Court extended constitutional
protection also to a dissident group that has been at the

center of many free-speech controversies, the Jehovah's Witnesses, a missionary group that seeks converts among many people who regard their views as anathema. Many city ordinances adopted in the 1920s and the 1930s prevented the Jehovah's Witnesses (or the International Bible Students, as they were known in the 1920s) from distributing tracts in residential neighborhoods. Sometimes whole cities were declared off limits. In one of the cases that reached the Supreme Court, a Witness stopped two men, both Catholics, on the street of a Catholic neighborhood in New Haven and asked permission to play a phonograph record for them. The men agreed to listen. The record, *Enemies*, bitterly attacked the Catholic religion. The listeners had the Witness arrested for inciting a breach of the peace. The Supreme Court unanimously reversed this conviction. Anti-Catholic views could not be excluded from a Catholic neighborhood, said the Court, and it could not be made a crime to state those views to Catholics.

In labor-organizing efforts, another major focus of free-speech battles before World War II, communities often attempted to resist by restricting the right of organizers to enter their communities, to speak publicly, or to organize demonstrations.

Some of the most dramatic free-speech battles were fought by the Industrial Workers of the World (or "Wobblies"). Organized in Chicago in 1905, the IWW was a radical organization, perceived by most Americans as a threat to society as they knew it. "We are here to confederate the workers of this country into a working-class movement," said Big Bill Haywood at the IWW's founding meeting, "in possession of the economic powers, the means of life, in control of the machinery of production and distribution without regard to capitalist masters." Said Eugene V. Debs, "The Industrial Workers is organized not to conciliate but to fight the capitalist class." The preamble to the IWW constitution stated this philosophy in especially stirring words: "The working class and the employing class have nothing in common. There can be no peace so long as hunger and want are found among millions of working people and the few, who make up the employing class, have all the good things of life. Between these two classes a struggle must go on until the workers organize as a class, take possession of the earth and the machinery of production, and abolish the wage system."

When the Wobblies came to town, the solution, as many elected officials saw it, was to deny them the right to speak. In 1908, in Spokane, Washington, all street meetings were banned. A Wobbly, John Panzer, who later served five years in prison for exercising free speech in defiance of the World War I Espionage Act, recalled the Spokane incident in his memoirs. "At one time," said Panzer, "we had the city jail, the county jail, the Franklin School House full, and a United States fort had eighty-five prisoners in it. The rank and file who spoke on the streets got thirty days for violation of the city ordinance, the leaders got six months in the county jail under the state conspiracy law." Aberdeen, Washington, Fresno and San Diego, California, and many other western cities took similar precautions, but the bloodiest battle took place in Everett, Washington, in November of 1916.

To protest repression of free speech in Everett, 260 Wobblies crowded on the steamship *Verona* and another 38 followed on another boat for the trip across Puget Sound from Seattle. They thought that their numbers would deter interference with their right of peaceable assembly. Leaflets had been distributed in Everett advertising their purpose. The *Verona* was met at the dock in Everett by the sheriff and an armed posse of vigilantes who fired at the men as the ship pulled in. Five Wobblies and two vigilantes were killed, thirty-one Wobblies and nineteen vigilantes were wounded, and seven Wobblies were missing, probably drowned. Two hundred and ninety-seven Wobblies from the boats and from Everett were arrested. Seventy-four were eventually tried for murder. After the acquittal of their leader, charges against the rest were dismissed.

The view that a town had the power to keep out a public assembly by a labor union or any other group persisted for many years. Mayor Frank ("I am the law") Hague of Jersey City, New Jersey, had attempted in the 1930s to exclude from the city he controlled those whose views he hated. The Congress of Industrial Organizations was Communist controlled, according to Hague, and therefore it could not hold public meetings in Jersey City. Such opponents of Hague's rule as Norman Thomas were forbidden to speak in the city, too. Even when Thomas tried to speak in a Newark park that adjoins Jersey City, his meetings were disrupted by Hague goon squads.

The American Civil Liberties Union brought a lawsuit to challenge Mayor Hague's power to banish from the streets of Jersey City those whose views he disliked. The case went to the United States Supreme Court and the resulting decision in 1939 became a landmark in the history of American constitutional law. "Wherever the title of the streets and parks may rest," said the Court in *Hague* v. *Committee for Industrial Organization*, "they have immemorially been held in trust for the use of the public and, time out of mind, have been used for purposes of assembly, communicating thought between citizens, and discussing public questions. Such use of the streets and public places has, from ancient times, been a part of the privileges, immunities, rights and liberties of citizens." The Supreme Court went on to say that the use of the streets could be regulated for comfort and convenience of citizens but this could not be a guise for denying any group the right to gather on the streets to speak out on public issues. In the forty years since *Hague*, unions have faced only sporadic legal interference with their right to organize.

When the United States Congress adopted the Smith Act in 1940, it was the federal government's first sedition law avowedly intended to apply in times of peace since the Sedition Act of 1798 had expired in 1801. Among its provisions, the Smith Act, which is still in effect, prohibits the advocacy of insubordination, disloyalty, mutiny, or refusal of duty in the military or naval forces of the United States as well as advocacy of the overthrow or destruction of any government in the United States by force or violence. Trotskyists, Communists, and Nazis have all been prosecuted under the Smith Act on charges that they advocated the forcible overthrow of the government of the United States.

As Zechariah Chafee, Jr. reported in his authoritative 1941 book, *Free Speech in the United States*, "The only opponents" of the act's sedition sections "were Osmond Fraenkel for the American Civil Liberties Union, Ralph Emerson for the C.I.O. Maritime Unions and Paul Schanenberg for the American Federation of Labor. The supporters of the sedition legislation tried to draw the usual red herring across the main issue of constitutional free speech by smearing the Civil Liberties Union as communistic." The bloodlust that characterized the congressional debate on the Smith Act prompted Chafee to write, "I never realized how Nazis feel toward Jews until I read what Congressmen say about radical aliens."

In July 1948, twelve officials of the Communist Party of the United States were indicted under the Smith Act for conspiring to advocate the duty and necessity of overthrowing the government of the United States by force. One of them, William Z. Foster, was not tried because of illness. The remaining eleven were convicted. Their appeal reached the U.S. Supreme Court in 1951, at the height of the post–World War II red scare that has become known as McCarthyism. The ACLU submitted an *amicus curiae* brief to the court asserting that the Smith Act was unconstitutional.

In deciding the case of *Dennis, et al.* v. *United States* (Dennis was one of the Communists), the Supreme Court said it was relying on the Holmes-Brandeis "clear and present danger" test. But in applying it, Chief Justice Vinson, who wrote the prevailing opinion, distorted its effect beyond recognition. "The mere fact that from the period 1945 to 1948 [the period covered by the indictment] petitioners' activities did not result in an attempt to overthrow the Government by force and violence is of course no answer to the fact that there was a group ready to make the attempt," said Vinson in his opinion for the Court.

The formation by petitioners of such a highly organized conspiracy, with rigidly disciplined members subject to call when the leaders, these petitioners, felt that the time had come for action, coupled with the inflammable nature of world conditions, similar uprisings in other countries and the touch-and-go nature of our relations with countries with whom petitioners were in the very least ideologically attuned, convince us that their convictions were justified on this score. And this analysis disposes of the contention that a conspiracy to advocate, as distinguished from the advocacy itself, cannot be constitutionally restrained, because it comprises only the preparation. It is the existence of the conspiracy which creates the danger. If the ingredients of the reaction are present, we cannot bind the Government to wait until the catalyst is added.

This interpretation of "clear and present danger" became a mainstay of the political repression that characterized the McCarthy period. In the six years after the *Dennis* decision, fifteen conspiracy prosecutions were brought against Communist Party officials and another ninety-six persons were convicted. In addition, several prosecutions were brought against individuals for membership in the Communist Party. By 1957, when the Supreme Court decided another Smith Act case, *Yates* v. *United States*, Earl Warren had replaced Vinson as Chief Justice and Justice John Marshall Harlan had joined the court. Harlan's prevailing opinion cut the ground from under the Smith Act prosecutions. His decision restored some meaning to the "clear and present danger" test. Ending the Smith Act prosecutions was more important than Senator McCarthy's death that same year in ringing down the curtain on the McCarthy era.

The damage done to political liberty by the *Dennis* decision demonstrates that interference with speech based on the allegation of "clear and present danger" must be rigorously limited to circumstances where a contrary voice has no chance to be heard before some great evil follows upon the direct urging of the speaker. If "we cannot bind the Government to wait until the catalyst is added," as Chief Justice Vinson maintained, then we cannot restrain the government from suppressing views that challenge its policies. If the decision in *Dennis* had not been eviscerated by *Yates*, great numbers of Smith Act prosecutions would probably have been brought against war resisters during the Vietnam War. They would have been prosecuted for conspiring in violation of the provision of the Smith Act that punishes advocacy of refusal of duty in the armed forces. By requiring greater proximity between advocacy and the evil to be prevented, *Yates* made such prosecutions much more difficult.

Right-wing fanatics were not feared in the McCarthy period as much as the Communists were. Even in 1949 the Supreme Court proved willing to uphold free speech for a rabid racist, Father Terminiello. A suspended Catholic priest, Terminiello denounced "Communistic Zionist Jews" and blacks in a speech to a crowd of sympathizers in a Chicago hall. Outside, as more than 1,000 antagonists of Terminiello demonstrated, police were unable to control the counterdemonstrators, who rioted and threw bricks, bottles, and stink bombs. After the speech, Terminiello was arrested and charged with inciting a breach of the peace.

The Supreme Court's decision, written by Justice William O. Douglas, said, "A function of free speech under our system of government is to invite dispute. It may indeed best serve its high purpose when it induces a condition of unrest, creates dissatisfaction with conditions as they are, or even stirs people to anger. Speech is often provocative and challenging. It may strike at prejudice and preconceptions and have profound unsettling effects. . . . That is why freedom of speech . . . is nevertheless protected against censorship or punishment, unless shown likely to produce a clear and present danger of a serious substantive evil that rises far above public inconvenience, annoyance, or unrest." In a strong dissent, Justice Robert Jackson protested that "there is a danger that if the Court does not temper its doctrinaire logic with a little practical wisdom it will convert the constitutional Bill of Rights into a suicide pact."

While Jackson's dissent was influential and his words about a "suicide pact" are often repeated, the *Terminiello* decision is a landmark case in ensuring that hecklers do not veto speech by their disorderly or violent response to a speaker. Those who riot or those who urge others to riot in circumstances where there is a "clear and present danger" of a riot may be punished. The punishment must not fall on speakers who remain peaceful themselves but whose words are so provocative that opponents riot.

The importance of this principle became manifest a decade later when blacks and whites began to demonstrate for racial equality in the South. Flouting the mores of Southern communities, they provoked extremely hostile reactions, often violent response. If violent reactions could stop civil rights demonstrations, the movement for racial equality would have been defeated at the start. Skokie's effort to stop the Nazis there by warning of violent response would, if supported by the courts, lead to suppression of civil rights or other peaceful protests and give the threats of unruly mobs a veto power over nonviolent demonstrators.

The leading court cases dealing with free speech for civil rights demonstrators are *Edwards* v. *South Carolina,* decided in 1963, and *Cox* v. *Louisiana,* decided in 1965. The *Edwards* case got started in March of 1961 when black high school and college students assembled at a church in Columbia, South Carolina, and about 200 of them marched in groups of about 15 to the South Carolina State House grounds. Their purpose was "to submit a protest to the citizens of South Carolina, along with the Legislative Bodies of South Carolina, over feelings and over dissatisfaction with the present condition of discriminatory actions against Negroes, in general, and to let them know that we were dissatisfied and that we would like for the laws which prohibited Negro privileges in this State to be removed." For this offense, 187 students were convicted of breach of the peace because, the South Carolina courts maintained, their demonstration angered some members of the crowd of 200 to 300 white onlookers. The Supreme Court reversed the convictions. "As in the *Terminiello* case," said Justice Potter Stewart, writing for the majority, "the courts of South Carolina have defined a criminal offense so as to permit conviction of the petitioners if their speech 'stirred people to anger, invited public dispute, or brought about a condition of unrest.'"

In December 1961, twenty-three black students from Southern University were arrested in downtown Baton Rouge, Louisiana for picketing stores that maintained segregated lunch counters. Reverend B. Elton Cox, Congress of Racial Equality field secretary, led a demonstration the next day in which 2,000 Southern University students staged a protest march in front of the state capitol building in Baton Rouge. Cox kept the students orderly during the demonstration. Then, at about noon, he addressed them and said, "All right. It's lunchtime. Let's go eat. There are twelve stores we are protesting. A number of these stores have twenty counters; they accept your money from nineteen. They won't accept it from the twentieth counter. This is an act of racial discrimination. These stores are open to the public. We are members of the public. We pay taxes to the federal government and you who live here pay taxes to the state." Cox was arrested and convicted of disturbing the peace.

This speech, the Baton Rouge Sheriff said at Cox's trial, was "inflammatory." It had produced "muttering" and "grumbling" by the white onlookers. But the Supreme Court overturned the conviction, with Justice Arthur Goldberg writing the majority opinion. As in the *Edwards* case, the *Terminiello* precedent was relied upon by the Supreme Court to overturn the conviction of a civil rights demonstrator. Just as Terminiello could not be punished for provocative speech that stirred unrest and invited dispute, Cox could not be convicted for remarks that made white onlookers mutter and grumble. The Louisiana law under which Cox was charged, said Justice Goldberg, was as "likely to allow for conviction for innocent speech as was the charge of the trial judge in *Terminiello*. Therefore, as in *Terminiello* and *Edwards* the conviction under this statute must be reversed . . . in that it sweeps within its broad scope activities that are constitutionally protected free speech and assembly."

The pretext of listener hostility was employed constantly by opponents of the black civil rights movement of the 1960s to suppress its demonstrations. Perhaps the most dramatic incident took place in Selma, Alabama, in 1965 where the Reverend Martin Luther King, Jr., led a campaign for voting rights. On March 7, five hundred civil rights demonstrators set out from Selma to march to the state capital, Montgomery. As they started out over the Edmund Pettus Bridge across the Alabama River to get on to the highway to Montgomery, Alabama state troopers charged at them swinging clubs and bullwhips. John Lewis of the Student Nonviolent Coordinating Committee suffered a fractured skull and dozens of other marchers were seriously injured. Governor George Wallace announced that the troopers had acted because the marchers could not be protected against angry whites waiting along the route to Montgomery. The day after the beatings on the Edmund Pettus Bridge, lawyers for King's Southern Christian Leadership Conference went to federal court seeking an order against Wallace and his troopers and protecting their right to march. "There just had to be a march," said Andrew Young, then one of King's top aides, "some kind of nonviolent demonstration to get the expression out. If there wasn't, you would have had real violence. You just can't turn off the spigot, not in a religious movement where confronting wrong is absolutely fundamental."

In federal court, King's group came before Judge Frank Johnson, who issued an order directing Governor Wallace and other state officials to protect the marchers. Judge Johnson also authorized the federal government to provide protection. Two days later, on Sunday, March 21, 3,000 marchers started out from Selma to Montgomery, protected by 1,800 U.S. Army military police and two Army helicopters. Near Montgomery, they were joined by other demonstrators; 20,000 took part in the final stages of the demonstration at the state capitol. Free speech had been vindicated in Alabama by a federal judge's rejection of the heckler's veto imposed by the governor. And Rev. Martin Luther King, Jr., transformed the disaster of the Edmund Pettus Bridge into a great triumphal procession for the civil rights movement.

Several of the post-World War II free speech cases decided by the United States Supreme Court have involved the First Amendment rights of racists. Aside from *Terminiello*, the most important such case the high court considered was an appeal from a Ku Klux Klan leader in Ohio who had been convicted under the state's law punishing "criminal syndicalism." The conviction was based on films made by a television cameraman showing a dozen hooded Klan members, some of them carrying guns. Another scene in the film showed Clarence Brandenburg, the Klan leader, making a speech. "This is an organizers' meeting," Brandenburg said in the film. "We have had quite a few members here today which are—we have hundreds, hundreds of members throughout the state of Ohio. I can quote from a newspaper clipping from the Columbus, Ohio, *Dispatch*, five weeks ago Sunday morning. The Klan has more members in the State of Ohio than does any other organization. We're not a revengent [sic] organization but if our president, our Congress, our Supreme Court continues to suppress the white, Caucasian race, it's possible that there might have to be some revengeance [sic] taken." In a second film, Brandenburg repeated these remarks and added, "Personally I believe the nigger should be returned to Africa, the Jew returned to Israel." Because he had advocated violence— "there might have to be some revengeance taken"—Brandenburg was sentenced to one to ten years in prison by the Ohio courts.

The Supreme Court was unanimous in reversing Brandenburg's conviction. "The constitutional guarantees of free speech and press," said the high court in a 1969 *per curiam* opinion, "do not permit a state to forbid or proscribe advocacy of the use of force or of law violation except where such advocacy is directed to inciting or producing imminent lawless action and is likely to produce such action." Once again, the decision proved beneficial to people with views diametrically opposed to those of Brandenburg. Later in 1969, the First Circuit Court of Appeals reversed the convictions of Dr. Benjamin Spock, the Reverend William Sloane Coffin, and their fellow defendants in the prosecution that had been the most dangerous interference with the free speech of opponents of the war in Vietnam. They had been convicted of conspiring to counsel young men to evade service in the armed forces. In reversing the convictions, the court of appeals relied on the version of the "clear and present danger" test set forth by the Supreme Court in *Brandenburg*. While Spock and the others opposed the war vigorously and counseled against military service, lawless action did not imminently follow their speech. Young men had an opportunity to consider other points of view before making decisions to resist the draft.

In a society of laws, rights won on behalf of hate-mongering racists such as Terminiello and Brandenburg are of direct value to civil rights demonstrators and war opponents. The reverse is also true. Deny free speech to Frank Collin in Skokie today and people with contrary views will lose some of their freedom. The Communist Party leaders convicted in the *Dennis* case were no champions of freedom. But the denial to them of freedom of speech was the key in permitting the repression of the 1950s. Many non-Communists and anti-Communists also suffered from McCarthyism. History is clear. The freedom of our enemies must be defended if we are to preserve our own freedom.

7

"They Have Rights?"

"Rights? They have rights?" Rabbi Meir Kahane asked at a Skokie synagogue. "What person has the right to demand that others be put into ovens?"

Rabbi Kahane is a street fighter. He does not believe in defending his enemies. But his questions eloquently state part of the case against permitting the Nazis to march in Skokie. To apply a test that the courts have employed in considering sexual materials, what the Nazis have to say is utterly without redeeming social value.

"Free speech, as originally conceived," said an editorial in the *Washington Star*, "was not designed, after all, to foist on us the mischief of guttersnipes, but to protect the community from official suppression of valuable ideas—ideas of conceivable truth, ideas deserving close consideration. 'Truth' was Milton's word for such ideas, but truth is a commodity in which the American Nazis, like their forerunners in Germany, have no interest. Their stock is evil myth and slanderous falsehood, identifiable as such by every civilized instinct. If this distinction cannot be made, what can be?"

In insisting that distinctions can be made, the *Star* was

responding to those advocates of free speech who point to the difficulty in determining which speech is to be permitted and which speech is to be forbidden. Perhaps there are borderline cases, they say, but that is not our problem in considering the Nazis. Wherever one draws the line, the Nazis are in the farthest corner of the far side of it. Hard cases may come along. It may be very troublesome to decide who may speak. But American Nazis have forfeited any claim to consideration of their views by civilized society by proclaiming that they stand for the same philosophy as those Nazis who put people into ovens. Anybody with any sense at all can distinguish between a Nazi and someone intent on expressing an idea that may not be in accord with established beliefs but nevertheless deserves to enter the stream of public debate. So goes the case against defending the enemy.

Speech has never been absolutely protected against governmental interference, these opponents say. They quote the United States Supreme Court decision in *Chaplinsky* v. *New Hampshire* in 1942: "It is well understood that the right of free speech is not absolute at all times and under all circumstances. There are certain well-defined and narrowly limited classes of speech, the prevention and punishment of which have never been thought to raise any constitutional problems. These include the lewd and obscene, the profane, the libelous, and the insulting or 'fighting' words —those which by their very utterance inflict injury or tend to incite an immediate breach of the peace. It has been well observed that such utterances are no essential part of any exposition of ideas, and are of such slight social value as a step to truth that any benefit that may be derived from them is clearly outweighed by the social interest in order and morality." Fighting words are as lethal as weapons, the argument goes.

Even if it were conceded that the Nazis are free to speak and to demand that Jews be put in ovens, it is argued that they should not be allowed to do so in Skokie. The

Nazis are not going to Skokie to seek adherents for their views. They hope to exploit the victims of Nazi terror who have sought refuge there by provoking a confrontation that will attract nationwide attention to the Nazis. "By their very utterance," the words of the Nazis, the *Chaplinsky* court would put it, "inflict injury" on the residents of a community that is a haven for survivors of the Holocaust. Residents of Skokie saw members of their own families tortured and murdered. They themselves suffered privations that should be unimaginable in a civilized society. The murderers were Nazis wearing swastikas. Must the suffering of the Holocaust survivors be renewed by exposure to the obscenities of a new generation of Nazis seeking publicity at their expense?

The Supreme Court noted in *Chaplinsky* that the libelous has never been protected by the doctrine of freedom of speech. Individuals have remedies in law when libelous statements are directed against them. The Nazis libel all the members of a race, religion, or a community. Why, ask opponents of the right to march, shouldn't members of a group defamed have some method of restraining those who defame them?

Supreme Court Justice Robert Jackson stated the case for laws prohibiting group defamation in a dissenting opinion in 1951. Racial and religious slurs "are not the kind of insult that men bandy and laugh off when the spirits are high and the flagons are low. They are not in that class of epithets whose literal sting will be drawn if the speaker smiles when he uses them. They are always and in every context insults which do not spring from reason and can be answered by none. Their historical associations with violence are well understood both by those who hurl and those who are struck by these missiles. Jews," said Jackson, who had returned to the Court after a leave in which he presided over the trials of Nazi war criminals at Nuremburg, "many of whose families perished in extermination furnaces in Dachau and Auschwitz, are more than tolerant if they pass off lightly the suggestion that unbelievers in Christ should all have been burned."

The following year, the United States Supreme Court upheld an Illinois law punishing group defamation enacted in 1917 in the immediate aftermath of race riots in two of the state's cities, East St. Louis and Springfield. That law was the model for one of the 1977 ordinances adopted by Skokie:

> *It shall be unlawful for any person, firm or corporation to manufacture, sell, or offer for sale, advertise or publish, present or exhibit in any public place in this state any lithograph, moving picture, play, drawing or sketch, which publication or exhibition portrays depravity, criminality or unchastity, or lack of virtue of a class of citizens, of any race, color, creed or religion which said publication or exhibition exposes the citizen of any race, color, creed or religion to contempt, derision, or obloquy or which is productive of breach of the peace or riots. . . .*

Skokie's principal amendment to this language was to proscribe "markings or clothing of symbolic significance," which had the same effect as the other forms of communication listed in the Illinois law.

The Illinois group libel law had been challenged by Joseph Beauharnais, a white supremacy agitator, convicted for distributing leaflets at a meeting of the White Circle League which defamed the Negroes of Chicago. When his appeal of that conviction brought the case to the United States Supreme Court, the Court divided five to four in upholding the constitutionality of the group libel law. Justice Felix Frankfurter—a founder of the American Civil Liberties Union, opponents of our stand take care to note—wrote the opinion for the majority:

It is not within our competence to confirm or deny claims of social scientists as to the dependence of the individual on the position of his racial or religious group in the community. It would, however, be arrant dogmatism, quite outside the scope of our authority in passing on the powers of a State, for us to deny that the Illinois Legislature may warrantably believe that a man's job and his educational opportunities and the dignity accorded him depend as much on the racial or religious group to which he willy-nilly belongs, as it does on his own merits. This being so, we are precluded from saying that speech concededly punishable where immediately directed at individuals cannot be outlawed if directed at groups with whose position and esteem in society the affiliated individual may be inextricably involved.

The special danger of group defamation, opponents of permitting the Nazis to march point out, is that its effect is cumulative. The "clear and present danger" test for determining whether speech is to be permitted is irrelevant. A racial slur repeated once or twice may be relatively harmless. But when it is repeated many times over, its effect is corrosive. If we wait until there is a "clear and present danger" of violence against the people who are being defamed, this argument goes, it will be too late. The state must act to restrain the Nazis while they are weak and before they have a chance to repeat their slurs so often that it is impossible to stop the violence they incite.

Even Justice Oliver Wendell Holmes, Jr., we are reminded, recognized that there are limits to the freedom to speak. Indeed, it was Holmes who first said, "The most stringent protection of free speech would not protect a man in falsely shouting fire in a crowded theater and causing panic." This test for limiting speech recognized that the character of speech is affected by the circumstances in which it takes place. A man standing by himself in the desert and yelling fire causes no panic and should not be punished for his actions. But in a crowded theater, the same words have a very different effect. Skokie is that crowded theater and the Nazis, with their armbands and their presence, a cry of fire. The Nazis want to preach that Jews should be put in ovens in just the place where their words would cause panic among people who still suffer from nightmares because they saw their families shoved into ovens. So the Nazis go to Skokie. Justice Holmes' argument that, "the best test of truth is the power of the thought to get itself accepted in the competition of the market" is rejected by those who argue against defending the enemy. George Will, in a column in the *Washington Post*, said that the market is no test of truth; it "measures preferences (popularity), not truth. Liberals say all ideas have an equal right to compete in the market. But the right to compete implies the right to win. So the logic of liberalism is that it is better to be ruled by Nazis than to restrict them."

Even some of those who may accept the Holmes view that the marketplace will test truth, question whether we must allow an idea to compete long after it has been proven false. The Nazis murdered 6 million Jews and millions of non-Jews. We fought a world war against them. We condemned them and their views at Nuremberg. After all that, can we not declare that Nazism has been tested in the marketplace and found wanting and deny it the right to prolong the competition?

George Will also suggests that the United States Constitution is intended to promote certain political ends. Rather than expect truth to emerge from the competition of ideas, Will asserts, the founders of our system of government believed, as they said in the Declaration of Independence, that certain truths are "self-evident." Government must remain faithful to these self-evident truths. Freedom of speech, yes, but only, says Will, "for all speech that does not injure the health of the self-evidently proper kind of polity, a republic."

George Will's argument for restricting speech is similar to a position advanced more than twenty years earlier by the political scientist Ernest van den Haag. "The fathers of our Constitution," he said, "were successful in protecting us against a government that might keep itself in power by taking away our rights. Less attention was paid to the possibility that some citizens might *give away* their democratic birthright and invite others to do so, as large groups abroad have done. Yet if our right to choose the government freely is *inalienable*, then we are not entitled to *give* the right away any more than the government is entitled to *take* it away. We cannot then elect a government that does not recognize the right of the people to oust it peacefully or that denies the necessary civil liberties. Nor, if freedom is to be inalienable, can invitations to alienate it be recognized as a legitimate part of the democratic process."

Professor van den Haag's views expose the irony in attempting to protect freedom by extending it to those who would use it to take away freedom. We have no right to sacrifice freedom for all others and for all time by making it possible for anyone to use freedom to abolish freedom. "The Constitution," as Justice Jackson warned, "is not a suicide pact."

Opponents of defending the rights of the enemy point out that the Nazis do not merely insist on their right to advocate freely denials of freedom to others, they also want police protection. By seeking out a place where they are as unwelcome as in Skokie, they force the community to guard them against violence if a riot is to be prevented. "If I decided that I wanted to stand outside Wally's Polish Pump Room this Saturday night," observes Chicago columnist Mike Royko, "and shout that everybody who eats Polish sausage is a pig, I suppose that would be my constitutional right. . . .

However, I don't think I should expect the city to give me a police escort when I got there.

"I'd have to take my chances. And if everybody in the place hit me with a beer stein, that is a risk I would have to consider before expressing my unpopular opinion. . . . The Nazis think it would be great fun to go Jew-baiting. Then let them go. However, they should have to face the normal risks that go along with looking for trouble just for the malicious fun of it."

There was a secondary issue in the debate: whether the American Civil Liberties Union itself should defend the Nazi right to march. Some opponents appear to concede that the Nazis have a right to march but maintain that the ACLU, given its limited resources, should not have provided the Nazis with legal representation. The ACLU, they correctly point out, turns away a great many cases in which civil liberties have been denied simply because it is unable to find the lawyers to handle them and unable to pay the costs of the litigation. Why, therefore, permit any part of the ACLU's scarce funds to be wasted by the Nazis?

Because ACLU members quit by the thousands after Skokie, taking on the Skokie case made the ACLU even less able to provide legal representation to other people whose civil liberties have been denied. By defending the Nazis, therefore, the ACLU is hurting a great many other more worthy people whose civil liberties are violated, so the charge runs.

Some see the defense of free speech for the Nazis not only as a waste of limited means but as a betrayal of the ACLU's function. "The overriding purpose of the ACLU," said economist Abba P. Lerner in a letter printed in the *New York Times*, "is to promote and defend a democratic social order in which freedom of speech is secure. If this purpose comes into conflict with freedom of speech directed at destroying such a social order, their obligation is surely to protect the social order of free speech rather than the free speech of its destroyers."

Some critics were especially offended by the fact that the attorney who defended the Nazis in court in the Skokie case, David Goldberger, is a Jew, and that other Jews (I among them) were prominently identified with defense of the rights of Nazis. "There seemed something fundamentally unseemly," said a prominent Cleveland Rabbi, Daniel J. Silver, in a sermon on the Skokie case, "about a group of Jewish lawyers, financed by a membership which is heavily Jewish, defending the rights of a few punks to go into a Jewish area and shout from the rooftops that it was too bad that Hitler did not finish the job."

8

The Risks of Freedom

"If there be any among us who would wish to dissolve this Union or to change its Republican form," Thomas Jefferson said in his first inaugural address, "let them stand undisturbed as monuments of the safety with which error of opinion may be tolerated where reason is left free to combat it."

Jefferson's words expressed the belief of the authors of the American constitutional system of government that the new republic should allow even its enemies to express their opinions. Against even the most venomous doctrines the republic had a strong antidote: the freedom to speak in opposition.

Freedom of speech permits a Rabbi Meir Kahane to lead a march of helmeted members of the Jewish Defense League chanting "Death to all Nazis" and "Kill the Nazis." Freedom of speech also permits a Frank Collin to advocate killing all Jews and blacks. Freedom of speech permits those who despise both the Nazis and the JDL to say so with all due vehemence. All may advocate freely even those things that would be illegal if carried into action. Freedom of speech is for the vicious as well as for the virtuous. So long as no restraints are placed on public debate, Jefferson's inaugural speech expressed confidence that virtue will prevail.

The faith that inspired Jefferson was never stated more forcefully and more eloquently than by the British poet and statesman John Milton. "Though all the winds of doctrine were let loose to play upon the earth," Milton wrote in 1644, "so Truth be in the field, we do injuriously by licensing and prohibiting, to misdoubt her strength. Let her and Falsehood grapple; who ever knew Truth put to the worse, in a free and open encounter? Her confuting is the best and surest suppressing. . . ."

Milton's certainty in the triumph of truth so long as the encounter is free and open was based on confidence in those who are exposed to this clash of doctrines. Any restriction on speech, said Milton, is a reproach against common people, "for if we be so jealous over them, as that we dare not trust them with an English pamphlet, what do we but censure them for a giddy, vicious, and ungrounded people; in such a sick and weak state of faith and discretion, as to be able to take nothing down but through the pipe of a licenser."

The founders of the American constitutional system shared Milton's confidence in the people who are exposed to a clash of doctrines and in the democratic institutions they established to carry out the will of the people. They placed the control of government in those people, the governed. The government derives its powers from the consent of the governed. Without their consent, the government lacks any just powers. With their consent, the government's powers exceed greatly those it derives from its military and police might. The government enjoys legitimacy because we have chosen it freely and, therefore, it can count on its citizens to aid it against its enemies from within as well as from without.

How are the governed to give their consent? By their

participation in the political process. By supporting candidates for office, running for office, voting, and through the exercise of free speech in formulating opinions on issues and candidates. The process does not end once a choice of candidates is made. The governed engage in a constant dialogue with their government. The government must listen to the people and respond to them. If the response is inadequate, the people may throw out the rascals and, through the formation of a new majority, choose new governors. We do not allow those who make up a majority at any moment to suppress speech and so to perpetuate themselves in power. The Constitution guarantees to the people not only the freedom to speak but the freedom of the press and the freedom to assemble peaceably to speak in concert with others who want to express similar views.

A faith that truth and virtue will prevail through free and open encounters with falsehood and evil may appear naive. But Jefferson and Milton were anything but naive. Although they understood the risks of freedom, they knew that it is far more dangerous to entrust the government with the power to determine what doctrines may be safely expressed by the people. Government can not claim to enjoy the consent of the governed if it places restraints on what they say. Only a society that permits people to speak can justly impose on them the decisions of the majority. The rule of the majority has no claim on the loyalty of the minority unless the minority has its chance to influence others and, thereby, to become the majority. How can we know if the minority has truth and virtue on its side unless its views are permitted to grapple with others in a free and open encounter? How can we suppress violence by minorities unless our government enjoys the legitimacy that derives from the consent it has obtained from the governed?

Because the courts recognize the connection between the freedom to speak and self-government, they give the widest latitude to speech on public issues. Other categories of speech, those that are irrelevant to self-government, enjoy less protection. The 1942 case of *Chaplinsky* v. *New Hampshire*, which became the principal precedent relied on by opponents of permitting the Nazis to march in Skokie, is regarded as a low point of judicial protection of the freedom to speak. Even the *Chaplinsky* court, however, in enumerating "certain well-defined and narrowly limited classes of speech" that did not enjoy constitutional protection, attempted to justify the exclusion of the "lewd and obscene, the profane, the libelous, and the insulting or 'fighting' words," by asserting that these are irrelevant to self-government. "Such utterances," the Supreme Court said, "are no essential part of any exposition of ideas, and are of such slight social value as a step to truth that any benefit that may be derived from them is clearly outweighed by the social interest in order and morality."

In the nearly four decades since *Chaplinsky*, the Supreme Court reviewed many cases in which the forms of speech it considered outside constitutional protection in 1942 were employed to deal with public issues. Take, for example, the Supreme Court decision in *Cohen* v. *California*. The 1971 case involved a young man, Paul Robert Cohen, who walked into a Los Angeles courthouse wearing a jacket decorated with the words "Fuck the Draft." Cohen was convicted of a breach of the peace. The *Chaplinsky* court would have regarded the words on Cohen's jacket as "lewd and obscene" or as "profane," and would have upheld his conviction. But because Cohen was using the words to communicate views on a public issue, the Supreme Court of 1971 found the wearing of the jacket constitutionally protected. Similarly, in 1964, in the case of *New York Times Company* v. *Sullivan*, the Supreme Court found that libelous statements enjoyed constitutional protection if they were directed against public officials and dealt with public issues. And in 1972, in the case of *Gooding* v. *Wilson*, the Supreme Court made clear that the "fighting words" exception to free speech could not be used to punish insults directed against large groups of people. Gooding was convicted by a lower court of saying to a police officer, "White son of a bitch, I'll choke you to death" and "White son of a bitch, I'll kill you." The Georgia law under which he was prosecuted outlawed "opprobrious words or abusive language." This was far too broad, in the view of the Supreme Court. The state could only punish "fighting words" under a law restricted to "those which have a direct tendency to cause acts of violence by the person to whom, individually, the remark is addressed."

The Illinois Appellate Court decided that the Nazis could be barred from displaying the swastika emblem in Skokie because the swastika constituted "fighting words," though the Illinois Supreme Court later overturned the decision. Should "fighting words" be outside the constitutional protection of free speech? Perhaps. But the term must be defined very narrowly. Sudden encounters between individuals in which one abuses and reviles the other and, thereby, provokes an immediate and unplanned violent response, involve such "fighting words." But "fighting words" should never be the basis for a prior restraint such as the Illinois Appellate Court imposed on the display of the swastika. If there is as much advance notice that provocative words will be spoken as it takes to get a court injunction, there is also enough notice to police a demonstration so as to prevent sudden violent outbursts. In the Skokie case, spectators at the demonstration would come knowing exactly what to anticipate. They would have no excuse for the unpremeditated violent reactions that the *Chaplinsky* court feared would take place in response to "fighting words" suddenly spoken to an individual.

The Illinois Appellate Court's decision that an emblem, the swastika, constituted "fighting words" also distorted that doctrine. An emblem conveys a message to a crowd and does not single out an individual for insult. It is not analogous to the one-to-one encounter at issue in *Chaplinsky*.

The Supreme Court's decision in *Beauharnais* v. *Illinois* is also frequently cited in support of banning the Nazi march in Skokie and, indeed, two of the ordinances adopted by Skokie were patterned after the law against group defamation upheld in the *Beauharnais* case. Even though the Supreme Court upheld the law, the legislature of Illinois later eliminated it from the state's revised statutes. One reason the law was repealed is that it appears to have been impossible to enforce. Although Illinois has had more than its share of bigots, the group-defamation law was almost never enforced in the half-century that it was on the Illinois statute books. The prosecution of Joseph Beauharnais was the only instance in which a prosecution under the Illinois group-defamation law reached an appellate court.

Legal philosopher Edmond Cahn, speaking of the Illinois group-defamation law in an address at the Hebrew University of Jerusalem in 1962, pointed out that if the law were enforced as written,

> *The officials could begin by prosecuting anyone who distributed the Christian Gospels, because they contain many defamatory statements not only about Jews but also about Christians; they show Christians failing Jesus in his hour of deepest tragedy. Then the officials could ban Greek literature for calling the rest of the world "barbarians." Roman authors would be suppressed because when they were not defaming the Gallic and Teutonic tribes they were disparaging the Italians. For obvious reasons, all Christian writers of the Middle Ages and quite a few modern ones could meet a similar fate. Even if an exceptional Catholic should fail to mention the Jews, the officials would have to proceed against his works for what he said about the Protestants and,*

of course, the same would apply to Protestant views on
the subject of Catholics. Then there is Shakespeare who
openly affronted the French, the Welsh, the Danes. . . .
Dozens of British writers from Sheridan and Dickens to
Shaw and Joyce insulted the Irish. Finally, almost every
worthwhile item of prose and poetry published by an
American Negro would fall under the ban because it
either whispered, spoke, or shouted unkind statements
about the group called "white." Literally applied, a
group-libel law would leave our bookshelves empty and
us without desire to fill them.

Proponents of group-defamation laws respond by asserting that prosecutors and judges have the necessary discretion
to apply such laws only to the likes of a Frank Collin or a
Joseph Beauharnais. This is the weakest possible argument
in favor of a group-libel law. It is a frank confession that
such laws cannot be written in ways that define with preci-
sion what speech should be prohibited. We must put our
trust, therefore, in the officials who enforce the laws and not
in the laws themselves.

Shortly before his death, Chicago's Mayor Richard
Daley showed how laws that purport to restrict objection-
able forms of speech are likely to be enforced. He announced his support for a proposal to prohibit depictions of
excessive violence in movies and on television. At a press
conference, Daley was asked to cite an example of a movie
that would be banned under the proposal he supported.
Medium Cool, he responded. *Medium Cool* is a documentary
film depicting the events surrounding the 1968 Democratic
Party Convention in Chicago. The only violence in the movie
is on the part of the Chicago police. They are shown beating
up antiwar and anti-Daley demonstrators.

Justice Holmes's assertion that "free speech would not protect a man in falsely shouting fire in a crowded theater and

causing panic" is the most frequently invoked argument for banning the Nazis from marching in Skokie. But the analogy that is drawn is very wide of the mark.

The analogy would be closer if, uninvited and without advance warning, the Nazis were to march into a Skokie synagogue during a service and to start chanting "Heil Hitler." Under such circumstances, the Nazis would take advantage of a captive audience—an audience that came together for purposes other than to listen to them. On the public street of Skokie, however, with ample notice that the Nazi demonstration will take place, only those who choose to observe the Nazis will be on hand. Only a handful of Skokie's 70,000 residents live close enough to the village hall so that they could witness the demonstration without a special trip to the site. Since it is a business district, few people are ordinarily on hand on a Sunday afternoon. If they do not want to see the Nazis, they have the option of leaving or turning away.

The shout of fire in a crowded theater when there is no fire is the antithesis of free speech. Reason is not free to combat it. No free and open encounter is possible between truth and falsehood. The panic takes place too quickly. Only one side can possibly be heard. The shout of fire takes place in circumstances where it creates what Justice Holmes called "a clear and present danger."

In Skokie, by contrast, free speech could operate. Many other points of view may be heard in addition to the views of the Nazis. Even if the Nazis should carry signs saying Jews should be put into ovens, there is no "clear and present danger" that anyone will act in accordance with this advice before reason has a chance to combat it.

Apprehension of a "clear and present danger" is never an excuse for prior restraint. As in the case of "fighting words," advance knowledge allows public officials to guard against danger. Moreover, because the residents of Skokie are so opposed to the Nazis, the circumstances that would create a "clear and present danger" are especially remote. If the Nazis marched in a neighborhood where they had large numbers of sympathizers, there would be a much greater likelihood of a "clear and present danger." In circumstances where a lynching is possible, for example, free speech would not protect a Nazi who said to a crowd of followers, "There's a Jew. Let's get him." Even if the speaker refrained from participating in the attack, the "clear and present danger" that violence would immediately result would permit the criminal prosecution of the speaker.

But, say those who would prohibit the Skokie march, isn't there a clear and present danger of violent reactions against the Nazis? Perhaps. But that cannot be the basis for prohibiting the Nazis from marching. If it were, any group of people who object to what a speaker has to say would suppress the expression of that view by threatening a violent reaction. They would enjoy what the late Harry Kalven called a "heckler's veto."

As free speech is practiced in the United States, speakers characteristically carry their messages to places where their views are anathema. Martin Luther King, Jr. marched in such racist communities as Birmingham, Alabama and Cicero, Illinois. Opponents of the war in Vietnam demonstrated in front of draft boards and military installations. Opponents of Nixon picketed the White House. The Jewish Defense League demonstrates in front of the Soviet Embassy. Anti-abortion demonstrators picket abortion clinics. Pro-abortion demonstrators picket Catholic churches. And so on.

Speakers and demonstrators go where they are not wanted in the hopes of attracting attention. There is drama inherent in the march of Martin Luther King, Jr., in Selma as there is drama in a Nazi march in Skokie. Dissenters know that the news media will pay attention when they create drama. If they do not, they have trouble getting access to the press to express their views to the general public. The effect, the late A. J. Liebling pointed out, is that freedom of the press belongs to anyone who owns one.

The same view was expressed some years later in Herbert Marcuse's influential essay, "Repressive Tolerance." Technology, says Marcuse, has concentrated the power to communicate in the hands of the few. "Effective dissent," he says, "is blocked where it could freely emerge: in the formation of opinion, in information and communication, in speech and assembly. Under the rules of monopolistic media —themselves the mere instruments of economic and political power—a mentality is created for which right and wrong, true and false are predefined wherever they affect the vital interests of the society." Truth, in Marcuse's view, has no chance to be heard if it conflicts with the interests of those who control access to communication.

Contemporary dissenters have discovered ways to make the communications media owned by others serve their purposes. They express their views in ways which capture the attention of the television cameras and the newspaper photographers. A demonstration in hostile territory is ideal for these purposes. So is the display of visually interesting symbols which can convey the message of the dissenters through a single photograph in a newspaper or through a few seconds of film footage on a television news program. And, as dissenters succeed in communicating their views to us, we have a chance to determine for ourselves whether truth and virtue are on their side or whether their views are false and vicious.

Dissenters also seek out hostile territory in order to test their opponents. If their opponents respond to peaceful dissent in an ugly and violent manner, those opponents may be discredited. Martin Luther King, Jr.'s movement thrived on displays of ugliness by Police Commissioner Bull Connor in Birmingham and Sheriff Jim Clark in Selma. The pictures that were flashed around the world of civil rights demonstrators being attacked by dogs, knocked down by water hoses, and tortured by cattle prods aroused sympathy for King's movement and repugnance against racist law-enforcement officers who responded violently to peaceful demonstrations.

By attempting to deny the Nazis the freedom to speak, Skokie itself served the Nazi cause. Frank Collin seemed to understand—at least intuitively—that if he could elicit from the residents of Skokie an ugly reaction to the Nazi march, it would also serve the Nazi cause.

Many advocates of constitutional rights regard the "clear and present danger" test as valueless in deciding questions of free speech. Its "effect upon our understanding of self-government has been one of disaster" said Alexander Meiklejohn in a series of lectures in 1947, subsequently published in his important book, *Political Freedom.* Meiklejohn points out that Justice Holmes, the formulator of this test, was quickly dissatisfied with it. Later in 1919, the same year that he discussed shouting fire falsely in a crowded theater, Holmes wrote, "I think we should be eternally vigilant against attempts to check the expression of opinions that we loathe and think to be fraught with death, unless they so imminently threaten interference with the lawful and pressing purposes of the law that an immediate check is required to save the country." As Meiklejohn observed, "The danger must be clear and present, but, also, terrific."

Justice Louis D. Brandeis, who had joined with Holmes in the two 1919 opinions, wrote an opinion eight years later in which Holmes joined and which attempted to limit further the "clear and present danger" test. "Those who won our independence by revolution were not cowards," said Brandeis. "They did not fear political change. They did not exalt order at the cost of liberty. To courageous, self-reliant men, with confidence in the power of free and fearless reasoning applied through the processes of popular government, no danger flowing from speech can be deemed clear and present, unless the incidence of the evil apprehended is so imminent that it may befall before there is opportunity for free discussion. If there be time to expose through discussion the falsehood and fallacies, to avert the evil by the processes of education, the remedy to be applied is more speech, not enforced silence."

The best consequence of the Nazis' proposal to march in Skokie is that it produced more speech, a great deal more. It stimulated more discussion of the evils of Nazism and of the Holocaust than any event since the Israelis captured Adolf Eichmann in Argentina in 1960 and brought him to Jerusalem to stand trial for war crimes.

The worst consequence of the Nazis' proposal to march in Skokie is that the arguments against permitting the march have fostered the impression that a community can assert that those whose views are anathema to it can be forbidden to enter its boundaries. It is not the first time a town or neighborhood has asserted such a power to exclude views it dislikes from its own "turf." The practice, however, had been largely discredited after Mayor Frank Hague lost his battle forty years ago to keep labor organizers out of Jersey City. Skokie revived the idea that it might be legitimate.

The most sophisticated argument against permitting the Nazis to speak is Ernest van den Haag's contention that "if freedom is to be inalienable . . . invitations to alienate it [cannot] be recognized as a legitimate part of the democratic process." The difficulty with this view is that it requires us to put our trust in government to determine who shall be denied the right to speak because it is their intention to take away freedom of speech. Unfortunately, governments have very bad records in making such determinations.

Recent American history provides us with an example of what happens when the approach espoused by van den Haag is put into practice. Stalin's labor camps were still operating in the 1950s. In any litany of twentieth-century obscenities, they run second only to Hitler's death camps.

Many Americans in the 1950s feared that if Communists came to power here, they would establish in the United States some equivalent of the Stalin regime in Soviet Russia. To prevent what van den Haag calls the alienation of freedom and to protect what Abba Lerner calls "a social order in which freedom of speech is secure," American governmental agencies denied freedom of speech to Communists.

Senator Joseph McCarthy and his colleagues who made decisions to deny freedom of speech to enemies of freedom did a clumsy job. They went after Stalinist Communists and anti-Stalinist Communists, people they regarded as fellow travelers and liberals they mistakenly identified as Communists.

Opponents of McCarthyism who only protested on grounds of mistaken identity were ineffectual. Once the concession is made that the enemies of freedom can be denied the freedom to speak, it is up to those in power to determine the identity of the enemies. If that power is to be curbed, it must be by insisting that it can never be exercised to limit the freedom to speak.

There are grave dangers in allowing the enemies of freedom the freedom to speak. But Milton and Jefferson understood that it is far more dangerous to allow government to deny the freedom to speak to the enemies of freedom. Almost inevitably, government confuses the enemies of its policies with the enemies of freedom.

As in the McCarthy days, freedom of speech can only be defended by resisting every incursion on the right to speak. The only social order in which freedom of speech is secure is one in which it is secure for everyone.

George Will's argument against the "marketplace of ideas"—that it "measures preferences (popularity), not truth" —carries even further. Democracy also only measures preferences. The idea of democracy, however, is not that a preferential system will always make the best choice of government. It is, rather, that when a government is chosen it will have the right to govern because it has the consent of the governed.

The marketplace of ideas is not a means for discovering eternal truths. If it could accomplish that, it would quickly make itself obsolete. The marketplace is, rather, a means to permit people to engage freely in the search for truth. They choose what doctrines to accept and what doctrines to reject. By being forced to compete with falsehood, truth is tested and strengthened. Truth is not allowed to degenerate into a tyranny that only has a hold on the minds of people because it is imposed on them. "Sometimes it is said," Thomas Jefferson noted in his first inaugural address, "that man cannot be trusted with the government of himself. Can he, then, be trusted with the government of others? Or have we found angels in the form of kings to govern him? Let history answer this question."

Those who assert that while the Nazis may have a right to speak they should enjoy no claim on the limited resources of the ACLU, ignore an operating principle of the organization. The ACLU does not turn away those whose freedom to speak has been violated. From its founding in 1920, the primary purpose of the American Civil Liberties Union has been to defend freedom of speech. Other concerns now consume most of the ACLU's resources. The ACLU takes on about six thousand court cases a year. It challenges political surveillance; opposes government secrecy; protects the right of people to count equally regardless of race, sex, sexual preference, or other status; challenges denials of rights to children, prisoners, mental patients, members of the armed services, farm workers, and the elderly; protects the right of privacy and the freedom to control one's own body; and so on. The ACLU also fights on behalf of the same causes in Congress and in state legislatures across the country.

Many of the ACLU's court cases require large resources. Complex evidentiary records must be compiled in challenging political surveillance by a government agency or in documenting abuses inside a prison or institution for the mentally retarded. Free-speech cases, however, rarely require the construction of voluminous evidentiary records. Civil liberties lawyers sometimes call them "paper" cases. The only legal work needed is the preparation of papers citing appropriate precedents and filing them in court. The comparatively slight drain on ACLU resources of a free-speech case would make false any assertion that the organization does not have the capacity to take on such matters. To reject any case because of the views of the client would be to acknowledge the power of government to place some ideas beyond the pale of constitutional protection. The ACLU, therefore, feels obliged to defend any group denied the freedom to speak. And if in the natural course of events a case falls to a Jewish lawyer, as the Skokie case did, it should be left with that lawyer. The ACLU should not exclude lawyers on racial or religious grounds any more than it should defer to the racial or religious likes and dislikes of prospective clients.

Many of the ACLU's battles in the noble cause of freedom of speech have been waged on behalf of despicable clients. It is not only that the great principles of Milton and Jefferson apply to them, too; it is also that abridgements of freedom are directed first against the most universally despised. It would be more pleasant for defenders of freedom to rally around the causes of a better class of victims. But if we wait until nice people are victimized, it may be too late. The first place to defend freedom is the first place it is denied.

9

England:
The Risks of Repression

"*Mein Kampf* is my doctrine," said John Tyndall in 1964. And in 1969, Tyndall expressed his view that "the Jew is like a poisonous maggot feeding on a body in an advanced state of decay."

These days, John Tyndall attributes his activities in Britain's National Socialist Movement and other Nazi organizations to "youthful indiscretions." But many Britons wonder whether maturity has changed Tyndall much. Although he now heads the National Front, an organization that rejects the Nazi label, the Front's overt racism and its political program make it fair to pin that label on it.

The National Front won 119,000 votes, or 5.5 percent of the total votes cast, in the Greater London council elections in May 1977. National Front candidates won a large enough vote to push the Liberal Party into fourth place in 32 of the 89 seats contested by both parties. In the East End of London, the National Front did especially well. In Bethnal Green and Bow, it won 19.2 percent of the vote, and it secured more than 10 percent of the vote in contests for ten East End council seats.

Outside London, the National Front has done even better in recent elections in such major cities as Birmingham and Leicester. Another right-wing political group, the National Party, has also become a significant factor in some British elections.

The National Front's success in Britain is attributable to popular resentment over the immigration of people of color from Commonwealth countries. In the mid-1960s, more than 100,000 people of Asian or African origin migrated to England each year. The British Commonwealth maintained the principle of *civis Romanus sum* of the ancient Roman Empire and no restrictions were placed on migration within the Commonwealth. By the late 1960s, however, that principle was abandoned. Work vouchers and other requirements were imposed to restrict immigration. Still the migrants came, though in reduced numbers. In 1976, Britain admitted 55,000 people of Asian and African descent from Commonwealth countries, and in 1977, 44,000.

In Britain, Parliament has the last word. It is not restrained by a constitution that limits its powers. A parliamentary law that restricts freedom of speech is only susceptible to challenge in Parliament itself. The best protection for civil liberty in Britain is tradition, but it is a tradition replete with instances in which freedom of speech and freedom of the press have been limited. Britons are denied a great deal of information about their government's activities by prosecutions under the Official Secrets Act and by threats of such prosecutions. The libel laws and the laws regulating public comment on judicial proceedings are also used extensively in Britain to mute discussion of public issues. Accordingly, the government's response to the National Front and predecessor groups has been to restrict their freedom to speak.

Several small Fascist groups modeled on Mussolini's party were organized in England in the 1920s. Their main political role was to turn up as counterdemonstrators against left-wing groups. Occasionally they would proffer their services as special police to deal with the labor strikes of the period. Those services were almost always rejected. Then Sir Oswald Mosley, a former Conservative Member of Parliament, pulled together those small Fascist groups in 1932 to form his British Union of Fascists. He took advantage of the unrest created by the Great Depression and organized mass meetings and demonstrations by his followers, who were known as Blackshirts. George Orwell, who attended a Mosley speech in 1936 along with about 700 other people, reported in his diary that "Mosley is a very good speaker. His speech was the usual claptrap—Empire free trade, down with the Jew and the foreigner, higher wages and shorter hours all around, etc, etc. . . . The blame for everything was put upon mysterious international gangs of Jews who are said to be financing, among other things, the British Labour Party and the Soviet. M's statement re the international situation: 'We fought Germany before in a British quarrel; we are not going to fight them now in a Jewish one' was received with loud applause." Mosley and his British Union of Fascists won political support in the same East End neighborhoods where the National Front got its largest vote four decades later.

Some of Mosley's meetings and demonstrations led to violent confrontations between the Blackshirts and their opponents. At a Mosley rally at London's Albert Hall in May 1935, there was a riot. Violence also marked a series of Fascist marches and demonstrations in London's East End in 1936. These incidents provoked Parliament to adopt the Public Order Act of 1936. The act made it a crime to use "in any public place or at any public meeting, threatening, abusive or insulting words with the intent to provoke a breach of the peace or whereby a breach of the peace is likely to be occasioned." The law also empowered the police to impose limitations as to time, place, and route on marches if the police believe such marches are likely to provoke a breach

of public peace or cause public disorder. If the police believe such measures insufficient, the 1936 law authorizes
them to request the council of a particular town or borough
to ban all marches. The Public Order Act of 1936 also prohibits the wearing in meetings and public places of uniforms
intended to express a political point of view. The law allows
nonpolitical groups such as the Boy Scouts and the Salvation Army to wear uniforms and it permits exceptions in
favor of political organizations for "ceremonial, anniversary
and other special occasions if the wearing of uniforms will
not be likely to involve risk of public disorder." The 1936 act
did not authorize any interference with meetings and rallies
other than marches.

Soon after the 1936 act was adopted, all marches were
barred in the East End of London. During World War II,
marches anywhere in the London metropolitan area were
prohibited. Mosley, by then an outspoken supporter of
Hitler, was imprisoned in 1940, the darkest time of the war.
The British authorities, fearing invasion, acted under wartime emergency powers legislation. Mosley was not released
until 1943, when the war's tide had turned and any threat of
invasion had abated.

When the war ended in 1945, a number of prominent
British artists and writers established the Freedom Defence
Committee to seek quick restoration of all civil liberties, with
a credo set forth in a statement signed by Benjamin Britten,
E. M. Forster, Augustus John, George Orwell, Herbert Read,
and Osbert Sitwell. "Threats to freedom of speech, writing
and action," they said, "though often trivial in isolation, are
cumulative in their effect and, unless checked, lead to general disrespect for the rights of the citizen. The Committee
gives aid to individuals or organizations irrespective of their
political views, the nature of the attack on their freedom
being the sole criterion on which it is determined whether
or not action should be taken. The Committee . . . works
for the abolition of the Emergency Powers Act, Defense

Regulations and all existing statutes restricting the freedom of political action."

Some of the members of the Freedom Defence Committee had previously been active in Britain's National Council for Civil Liberties, founded in 1934 and dominated by Communists in the World War II period. It had refused to defend civil liberties for Fascists and Trotskyists. Orwell and Forster were among those who resigned from the NCCL over its failure to defend civil liberties evenhandedly. When the NCCL regained its moorings and resumed defending civil liberties for all, the Freedom Defence Committee's reasons for existence disappeared and it expired.

From 1948 to 1950, the worst years of the cold war, a ban on marches was again imposed on the entire London metropolitan area. Ostensibly aimed also at Fascists, the ban's real target was Communists. In the years immediately following the war, when Fascist organizations were incapable of rallying support in Britain, communism was a powerful force in several West European countries and greatly feared by public officials in Britain.

As in the United States, political protest demonstrations were rare during most of the 1950s and there were few occasions to invoke the Public Order Act. That all changed toward the end of the decade. The Campaign for Nuclear Disarmament, organized in Britain in January 1958 with Bertrand Russell as its president, sponsored a march in 1959 from Aldermaston to Trafalgar Square in central London. It became an annual event. By February of 1960, the CND was able to assemble a crowd of 20,000 people for one of its rallies in Trafalgar Square and about 5,000 people followed Bertrand Russell from the square to the government buildings at Whitehall.

Although these meetings had been peaceful, the government began to invoke the Public Order Act against them. Marches and demonstrations were prohibited. Bertrand Russell was prosecuted for inciting violations of the law, convicted, and sentenced to two months in prison. Russell reports in his autobiography that when the sentence was pronounced, "cries of 'shame, shame, an old man of eighty-eight!' arose from the onlookers. It angered me. I knew that it was well meant, but I had deliberately incurred the punishment and, in any case, I could not see that age had anything to do with guilt. If anything, it made me the more guilty. The magistrate seemed to me nearer the mark in observing that, from his point of view, I was old enough to know better." Russell served a week of his sentence. Many of his followers served much longer periods in prison.

The Campaign for Nuclear Disarmament turned the prosecutions under the Public Order Act to its advantage. It deliberately engaged in nonviolent civil disobedience and its leaders exposed themselves to punishment in order to get attention, arouse sympathy, and win converts to their cause. The government escalated the charges it brought against the demonstrators—who remained nonviolent—and, in some cases, when it charged them under the Official Secrets Act, was able to send them to prison for periods of as long as eighteen months. While the sentences were painful, the CND succeeded in promoting worldwide protests against nuclear weapons. Its efforts paid off in the Nuclear Test Ban Treaty of 1962.

In 1965, Parliament adopted the Race Relations Act, making it a crime to incite racial hatred. That law was amended in 1976 and again in 1977. Under the recent amendments, there is no longer any requirement that intent be proven. The law in Britain now makes it an offense to distribute abusive, threatening, or insulting literature at public meetings or to use words likely to stir up hatred against any racial group.

Adoption of these laws has had no discernible impact on the National Front. Its leaders find it easy to avoid specific violations of the law while continuing on their course of exploiting British resentment of nonwhite immigrants.

Code words are easily substituted for explicit references to race. National Front speakers attack immigration and call for law and order. Everyone understands what they mean.

One prosecution under the Race Relations Act proved that nonenforcement—even when speakers are openly racist —would be in the best interests of the minorities the law is intended to protect. John Kingsley Read, a predecessor of John Tyndall as chairman of the National Front, was tried in January of 1978 for inciting racial hatred. Read had told an audience that he was under a court injunction prohibiting slurs against colored immigrants and, therefore, would talk about "niggers, wogs, and coons." Read also spoke of the death of a young Asian and said, "One down, one million to go." At the trial, the judge instructed the jury that the term *nigger* was harmless. When he attended schools in Australia, the judge said, he was nicknamed Nigger because he sang songs in an aboriginal language. The all-white jury acquitted Read; spectators in the courtroom greeted the decision with applause.

The National Union of Students, the organization that federates student unions at British universities, took action against the National Front in 1974. The NUS adopted a resolution saying that representatives of "openly racist and fascist organizations" were to be prevented from speaking on college campuses "by whatever means necessary (including disruption of the meeting)."

The following year, when the United Nations General Assembly adopted its resolution asserting that Zionism is racism, student unions at college campuses in Britain put into practice their 1974 resolution by disrupting speeches by Israelis and Zionists. One of those prevented from speaking on a college campus was the Israeli ambassador to England.

Nor has the campaign against Zionism on British college campuses stopped with the disruption of speeches. At one British university, the Jewish society was denied the funds it had previously received from the student union. The society's offense was that it had sponsored Israeli speakers. "The essence of racism is the mythical belief in race superiority," said a student union resolution that accompanied the cutoff in funds. "The South African racists, the Zionists and fascists share this belief in common. Each professes to be the Chosen People." At another university, the student union attempted to expel the Jewish society but was restrained by the university administration, producing a controversy over administration interference in student union affairs.

The National Front, a target of the 1974 resolution, found this turn of events very much to its liking. It distributed literature praising the student unions that took action against campus Jewish societies. An effort to interfere with free speech by Fascists had been transformed into an anti-Semitic campaign vigorously applauded by Fascists.

Jews were not the only non-Fascist victims of the NUS resolution. Some conservatives who are very far from being Fascists were also barred from college campuses. After Sir Keith Joseph was prevented from speaking, the *New Statesman* said that the National Union of Students "betrayed an infantile inability to distinguish fascists from maverick conservatives." Leaders of the NUS subsequently apologized for their actions against Sir Keith Joseph and, by December of 1977, decided that their whole campaign against Fascist and racist speakers was ill-advised. Endorsement by the National Front of the campus anti-Semitism inspired by their resolution proved too much for NUS leaders. The 1974 resolution was repealed at the NUS national conference in 1977 and, at the same time, a resolution was adopted asserting that any student union discriminating against a campus society on grounds of race, creed, or religion would be expelled from the national organization. The threat of expulsion was intended as a response to the student unions that had acted against campus Jewish societies.

The transformation of the NUS anti-Fascist campaign

into an anti-Zionist and then anti-Jewish campaign is attributable to the strength on British college campuses of the Arab student population, other "Third World" students, and Communists. The combination of the NUS resolution prohibiting racist speakers and the United Nations resolution on Zionism provided these opponents of Israel with the pretext for putting into practice their anti-Zionist campaign. It was a classic demonstration of the way that restrictions on free speech intended to aid racial and religious minorities are applied in a way that harms those minorities.

A new British organization known as the Anti-Nazi League has also suffered from restrictions on freedom of speech that were intended to apply to the National Front. Formed in November 1977, the ANL has proved a popular alternative to other groups that have opposed the National Front. Unlike the Socialist Workers Party, a Trotskyist group, the Anti-Nazi League does not seek direct physical confrontations with the National Front. Instead, it holds its own rallies and demonstrations. The ANL attracted 5,000 members in its first three months of operation and, by February 1978, sought permission to hold a major demonstration. The demonstration was banned under a public order that was intended to stop National Front demonstrations. By late April, however, ANL leaders had persuaded police to permit their demonstration to take place. When it did, 80,000 people gathered to participate in a rally and a four-mile march through London's East End, the site of the National Front's greatest electoral successes. It was a stirring occasion. The exercise of free speech by the Anti-Nazi League proved a powerful remedy for the infection spread by the National Front.

The British laws aimed at curbing the incitement of race hatred have also backfired. The code words to which the National Front has resorted to avoid violations of the law are more palatable for other political leaders to borrow than the cruder words that are now forbidden. Margaret

Thatcher, leader of the Conservative Party, has been particularly adept at borrowing the National Front's code
words. In a nationally televised interview in early 1978, she
complained that the British were being "swamped by people
of a different culture" and she promised "an end to immigration." By the end of the century, she said, there would be 4
million people of Asian and African descent in Britain, "an
awful lot. . . . Every country can take small minorities and
in some way they add to the richness and variety of this
country. The moment the minority threatens to become a
big one, people get frightened." In that interview, Mrs.
Thatcher went so far as to give the National Front credit
for its role in making an issue out of immigration. Mrs.
Thatcher's political tactics paid off in local elections in May
of 1978. The Conservative Party made gains and the National Front declined from the high point it had reached the
previous year. But the battle against racism did not gain. It
is far more dangerous when a major party engages in racist
politics, even though it uses polite language, than when a
minor party attracts attention through the use of ugly racial
epithets.

"An Englishman's relationship with authority is entirely
one-sided," says Tony Smythe, a prominent British civil lib-
ertarian and for eight years the general secretary of the National Council for Civil Liberties. "He is expected to trust in
those who operate the system: to count on their fairness,
accept their judgments, and defer to their wisdom." Lacking
any equivalent of the First Amendment, British citizens
whose freedom to speak has been curbed cannot challenge
the Public Order Act, the Official Secrets Act, or the Race
Relations Act. They can only resist and hope that the officials
charged with administering these laws will be wise and will
exercise self-restraint.

Despite the restrictions on liberty imposed under such laws,
Britain remains a free country. "Our freedom," Walter Bage-

hot pointed out more than a century ago in his classic essay, *The English Constitution*, "is the result of centuries of resistance, more or less legal, or more or less illegal, more or less audacious, or more or less timid, to the executive Government. . . . We look on State action, not as our own action, but as alien action; as an imposed tyranny from without, not as the consummated result of our own organized wishes." It is this tradition of resistance, exemplified by Bertrand Russell's civil disobedience, that is the nearest British substitute for the formal constitutional restraints that American dissenters can secure to limit the executive branch of their government. Public officials in Britain only infrequently exercise their power to restrict speech. It could happen more often if there were no resistance. As in the United States, race and war have been the principal issues that produced street demonstrations in Britain in the period since the end of World War II. But popular feeling on those issues in Britain has never become so heated as in the United States during the civil rights demonstrations and the antiwar demonstrations. Although in the United States feelings ran so high that people were killed in places such as Neshoba County, Mississippi and Kent State, no comparable violence has taken place in Britain.

Even though political strife has been much more subdued in England than in the United States, measures originally adopted to restrict speech by Fascists were employed to silence opponents of nuclear weapons, Zionists, and anti-Fascists. How would Lyndon B. Johnson, Richard M. Nixon, George C. Wallace, and Richard J. Daley have acted if they were armed with the powers of Britain's Public Order Act and if they faced no possibility of constitutional challenge? It is only possible to speculate. Given the turbulent street demonstrations American public officials confronted, it seems likely that the repression of liberty would have been far greater than any that Britain has experienced.

10

Weimar Germany:
Abandoning Moral Authority

Weimar Germany is frequently cited as an object lesson by opponents of permitting the Nazis to march in Skokie. It was a free and democratic society, the argument goes. The Nazis were able to take advantage of the freedom accorded to all citizens by the Weimar government in order to subvert freedom. "Don't think it can't happen here," say many of the letters I have received opposing my defense of the Nazis' right to march in Skokie. "Look what happened in Germany."

One parallel is that several Germans of Jewish descent were predecessors of Frank Collin in seeking prominence as Nazis. The dubious distinction of being the first probably belongs to a Count Anton Arco, who in early 1919 shot and killed Kurt Eisner, a writer, a socialist, and a Jew who had led a revolution and who had become the premier of Bavaria. Arco murdered Eisner on a main street of Munich in full view of a large number of witnesses.

The motive of the murder was apparently Arco's need to prove his courage to the members of the Thule Society, an organization named after the ancient Roman word for a mythical Nordic kingdom and an important predecessor of the Nazi Party. Alfred Rosenberg, later the Nazi Party's theoretician and one of its foremost anti-Semites, Rudolf Hess, and other Thule Society leaders had rejected Arco for membership because of his Jewish origins.

As matters went in the early days of the Weimar Republic, the Eisner murder was immediately avenged. Spartacists, left-wingers who named their organization after the leader of a slave revolution in ancient Rome, assaulted two Bavarian ministers, killing one, Rosshaupter, and seriously wounding the other, Auer.

Political murders were commonplace in Weimar Germany. A 1922 study by a statistician, Dr. Emil Gumbel, documenting political murders since the end of World War I, found that right-wing groups such as the Thule Society had committed 354 political murders and left-wing groups such as Spartacus had committed 22. According to Gumbel, 326 of the murders by right-wingers went unpunished. Light sentences were the rule when a right-winger was convicted of a political murder, but criminal prosecutions were brought in almost all of the murders by left-wingers and they resulted in ten executions. Left-wing assassins who escaped execution received long prison sentences.

The pattern for punishing right-wing political murders was set early when the two principal leaders of the Spartacists, Karl Liebknecht and Rosa Luxemburg, were assassinated in Berlin in January 1919. They were killed by members of a *Freikorps*, one of the paramilitary bands made up of ex-soldiers, most of them unemployed, who continued to fight wars in the streets of German cities after Germany was forced to sign an armistice with its World War I opponents. These *Freikorps* were among the elements that Hitler eventually brought together in the Nazi party. Their activities were not slowed down significantly by the punishments meted out for the Liebknecht and Luxemburg murders. One of the two *Freikorps* members convicted of the

murders, Runge, got a sentence of two years and two weeks
for "attempted manslaughter." The other, Vogel, got four
months simply for "failing to report a corpse and illegally
disposing of it." Vogel had thrown Rosa Luxemburg's dead
body into Berlin's Landwehr Canal. Before her death, she
had been beaten into unconsciousness and shot in the head.

Matthias Erzberger, the Weimar government's finance
minister, and Hugo Haase, leader of a major political party,
were among the victims of political murders. The most prominent of all victims of a political assassination was Walter
Rathenau, the foreign minister. Rathenau, a Jew, a wealthy
industrialist, a brilliant and dominant public personality,
and German's principal negotiator in several of the international conferences that followed the Versailles Treaty, was
murdered on June 24, 1922. "A new chapter of German history begins or at least should begin, as a result of this mur-
derous act," Rathenau's friend and biographer, Count Harry
Kessler, wrote in the diary that is one of the richest sources of
information on the politics and passions of Weimar Germany. The next day's entry in Kessler's diary reports, "A mass
demonstration in the Lustgarten. More than two hundred
thousand people, a sea of faces, over whose heads waved
countless red and black-red-gold flags. I was supposed to
speak but, as I am still hoarse, declined. Speeches were made
from various points: the Palace balcony, the Emperor William Memorial, and that to Frederick William III. A little
boy, with a black-red-gold flag, perched on the head of
Frederick William. The bitterness against Rathenau's assassins is profound and genuine. So is firm adherence to the
Republic, a far more deeply rooted emotion than prewar
monarchical 'patriotism' was."

Despite the outpouring of public emotion in response
to Rathenau's murder, things quickly went back to business
as usual. Just one week after Rathenau's funeral, Kessler's
diary entry reports, "Last night an attempt on Harden's life.

He is severely wounded." Maximilian Harden, another friend of Kessler, was a leading liberal journalist of the time.

A month after Rathenau's murder, the Weimar government adopted the *Gesetz zum Schutz der Republik*, an emergency Act for the Protection of the Republic. In addition to making conspiracies against the leaders of the republic a federal crime, the act also authorized the punishment of speech glorifying the perpetrators of such crimes or speech vilifying the institutions of the Republic. While the provisions of the act punishing conspiracies were only desultorily enforced, the Weimar government demonstrated some vigor in prosecuting offensive speech. This produced conflict between the Reich (federal) government and the government of Bavaria, where the Nazis were strongest.

The year after Rathenau's assassination, Adolf Hitler attempted his bloody "beer hall putsch" in the Bavarian capital, Munich. It had some of its origins in strife over enforcement of the Act for the Protection of the Republic. Hitler's storm troopers used machine guns in their attempt to stage a revolution. Fourteen people were killed in one brief exchange of fire between Hitler's men and the Munich police.

Despite the gravity of the offenses committed, a special court imposed minimal sentences on Hitler and the other leaders of the putsch. General Ludendorff, a World War I hero whose personal prestige had made possible the attempted putsch and who shared responsibility for it with Hitler, was acquitted entirely. Hitler received the minimum sentence of five years' imprisonment but only served eight and a half months. He was not confined in a prison with other criminals but served his sentence in pleasant circumstances where he was able to complete the writing of *Mein Kampf*.

On paper, the Weimar Republic was a free and democratic society. Its constitution was, in general, an admirable document, although the guarantees of rights in it were less than absolute. Article 118, for example, provided for freedom of speech only "within the limits of the general laws." The impression that Weimar was a free society is fostered by the great flowering of arts, music, and theater that took place in Berlin in the 1920s. But lacking a government with the will and the strength to enforce the provisions of the constitution and the laws against politically motivated violence, Weimar did not safeguard the liberties of Germans. The constitution itself was so lightly regarded that the Nazis didn't bother to repeal it when they took over. They left it in place but ignored it.

The Nazis did not defeat their political opponents of the 1920s through the free and open encounter of ideas. They won by terrorizing and murdering those who opposed them. A popular cabaret act of the period summed it up. The *Conferencier*, as the master of ceremonies was called, would tell a story about a law student taking an oral examination. A professor asks the student about the insanity plea as grounds for acquittal for murder. Why is the plea granted? The student looks puzzled. The professor begins coaching. "Come on. You read the papers. You know that every day, defendants are acquitted whose crimes have been proven. It is not because they acted in self-defense. It is because . . ." Slowly, the student catches on and, finally, responds brightly, "It is because they are Nazis."

While hundreds of Nazi political murders went unpunished, the Weimar government would occasionally prosecute those who were publicly critical of the descent into Nazism. As early as 1919, the painter George Grosz was charged with the crime of defaming the reputation of the army. With the help of the rich and influential Count Kessler, who was equally at home in the world of the arts as in government and politics, Grosz escaped punishment. Later, however, Grosz published the magnificent series of paintings and drawings for which he is best known, *Ecce Homo*, issued a decade before the Nazis came to power, yet capturing prophetically all the nightmare qualities of the gangster state to come.

For publishing *Ecce Homo*, George Grosz—Germany's greatest artist—was prosecuted and convicted under a group-defamation law that the Weimar government never invoked against the Nazis. Grosz paid a fine rather than go to prison. The government also confiscated many of the original plates for *Ecce Homo*.

The Weimar government demonstrated its lack of concern for freedom of speech also in its dealings with Germany's greatest playwright, Bertolt Brecht. He had produced a film, *Kuhle Wampe*, named after a Berlin slum. The film, eventually shown in the United States under the name *Whither Germany?*, depicted the lives of the unemployed. Showings of *Kuhle Wampe* were banned by the Weimar government because of a scene in which the suicide of a young worker is linked to the issuance of a presidential emergency decree. This, the government censor said, defamed the president of the Weimar Republic.

In 1925, the government of Bavaria banned speeches by Hitler. The ban backfired as the Nazis exploited it by distributing a drawing of Hitler gagged, with the caption, "One alone of 2,000 million people of the world is forbidden to speak in Germany." At a 1926 rally in Munich to celebrate Hitler's birthday, Julius Streicher spoke on "Why is Hitler not allowed to speak?" while Hitler stood by silently. The ban was soon revoked.

Weimar Germany, like Skokie nearly half a century later, attempted to combat Nazism by prohibiting the wearing of uniforms and emblems indicating political affiliation. Such prohibitions on uniforms, however, proved meaningless. Nazi political murders mattered, not Nazi uniforms.

The Weimar government perished in the same way that it began its life: unable to act against political violence. By

August 1932, the Nazis had captured 230 seats in the Reichstag, nearly 40 percent of the total. Their electoral successes, however, produced no moderation in their street tactics. As it had been from the start, terror was their instrument. "Assaults, bomb-throwings, and murders continue in East Prussia, Bavaria and Holstein," Count Kessler reported in his diary for August 5, 1932. "It has now been officially established that the use of arson and bomb-throwing at Königsberg were committed by Nazis. The government held a Cabinet meeting on the subject yesterday, but confined itself to threatening vigorous action. It obviously hesitates about getting on the wrong side of the Nazis."

Soon after the Nazis took power in Germany, the Dollfuss government in neighboring Austria adopted legislation outlawing its National Socialist Party and various local Nazi groups. The legislation proved to be ineffectual in preventing the rise of Nazi sentiment in Austria. Despite the attempt to suppress speech by Nazis, their ideas took hold so that much of the Austrian public welcomed the eventual *Anschluss* with Germany.

When the Nazis achieved power, they were quick to suppress freedom of speech. Hitler was appointed chancellor on January 30, 1933. A month later, the Reichstag burned. Hitler seized the occasion to procure an emergency decree from the aged president, Hindenburg, "for the Protection of People and State." It proclaimed, "Therefore restrictions on personal freedom, or the right of free speech, including freedom of the press, freedom of association and meetings; infringements on the secrecy of the mails, telegraphs and telephones; orders of home search and confiscation; as well as restrictions on the right of private property, even beyond the legal limits, are permissible." The Nazi government even reached out and tried to silence world Jewry by threatening that protests would make matters worse for the Jews of Germany. On April 2, 1933, Joseph Goebbels, clearly speaking for Hitler, said, "The more they [Jews in other countries] speak of it, the more acute becomes the Jewish question, and once the world begins to concern itself with this question, it will be solved to the detriment of the Jews." This tactic proved to be effective: Jewish leaders in other countries muted their voices for fear of making matters worse for their brethren in Germany. And by driving Jews out of professions where they could communicate with others—journalism, literature, theater, law, art, and education—the Nazis made sure that the Jews of Germany had little opportunity to speak out and draw attention to their plight.

The history of the Weimar Republic does bear study when we confront the reemergence of a Nazi movement in the United States. But that history does not support the views of those who say that the Nazis must be forbidden to express their views. The lesson of Germany in the 1920s is that a free society cannot be established and maintained if it will not act vigorously and forcefully to punish political violence. It is as if no effort had been made in the United States to punish the murderers of Medgar Evers, Martin Luther King, Jr., James Reeb, Viola Liuzzo, the three civil rights workers killed in Neshoba County, Mississippi, and the other victims of the effort in the 1960s to desegregate the Deep South. There would have been hundreds of additional murders if the federal government of the United States had not stepped in to bring prosecutions where local law-enforcement agencies evaded their duty. The South, and the rest of the United States, would not be a free society today if those prosecutions had not been brought.

Prosecutions of those who commit political violence are an essential part of the duty the government owes its citizens to protect their freedom to speak. Violence is the antithesis of speech. Through speech, we try to persuade others with the force of our ideas. Violence, on the other hand, terrorizes with the force of arms. It shuts off opposing points of view.

Did the American Nazis threaten violence in connection

with the Skokie march? No. The only threat of violence was by opponents of the Nazis against the Nazis. If the lesson of Weimar Germany means anything, it is that the government must act vigorously to prevent violence from any source—even from people with good motives. If violence occurs despite the best efforts of the government to prevent it, those who engage in violence should be prosecuted. In permitting Spartacists and the *Freikorps* to fight it out on the streets of German cities and to settle their scores with each other by avenging each other's murders, the Weimar government abandoned any claim it had to moral authority.

Columnist Mike Royko's solution to the Skokie problem —let the Nazis have their fling at Jew-baiting, provide no police protection, and let them take the consequences—has its attractions. And Royko's way with words enhances its appeal. No doubt, though, there were politicians in Nazi Germany who thought that the rival bands of Nazis and Communists who shot each other in the streets deserved each other and deserved to be shot by each other. A free and democratic society, however, uses its own strength to enforce the right to speak even of those who parade in the clothing of those who took advantage of the weaknesses of the Weimar Republic a half-century ago.

Epilogue

Sixteen months in which the Nazis had captured the attention of the nation ended on July 9, 1978. On that warm and humid Sunday, Frank Collin and about twenty-five uniformed followers held a rally in Marquette Park. A federal court's decision two weeks earlier granting the Nazis the right to demonstrate in that Chicago park had given them the excuse they sought for canceling the Skokie march at the last moment. Their exclusion from Marquette Park where they could exploit the racial tensions of the neighborhood had inspired their effort to march in Skokie.

The Nazi rally lasted less than an hour. A crowd of about two thousand people made so much noise that the speeches by Collin and his St. Louis Nazi comrade, Michael Allen, were all but drowned out. Some of the crowd shouted support for the Nazis and "Death to the Jews." Others reviled Collin and shouted "Death to the Nazis." The size of the crowd was swelled by the presence of several hundred plain-clothes police officers who broke up sporadic fights and arrested seventy-two persons, most of them charged with disorderly conduct, only a few with assault. Thanks to the police vigilance, no serious violence took place. The police also kept one group of anti-Nazis out of Marquette Park entirely. A number of anti-Nazis complained to the Illinois ACLU and secured its aid in bringing a lawsuit challenging interference with their First Amendment rights.

Hoping to create more Skokies, the Nazis announced plans for demonstrations in several other Chicago suburbs. That petered out, however, when only three Nazis showed up for one demonstration and the press virtually ignored it. The Nazis were on their way back to obscurity.

Remarkably, during those sixteen months, the Nazis gained no adherents. Although Skokie's attempt to deny the Nazis the freedom to speak had backfired, bestowing on them the opportunity to speak almost daily to the entire nation through the press, when it was all over no one had been persuaded to join them. They had disseminated their message and it had been rejected.

Why did the Nazi message fall on such deaf ears? Revolutionaries and advocates of destruction attract followers readily when the society they wish to overturn loses legitimacy. Understanding this process, revolutionaries try to provoke the government into using repressive measures. They rejoice, as the American Nazis did, when their rights are denied to them; they count on repression to win them sympathizers.

In confronting the Nazis, however, American democracy did not lose, but preserved its legitimacy. When the Chicago Park District and the village of Skokie denied the Nazis the right to speak, the courts intervened to protect that right. When the Nazis assembled in St. Louis, at the federal building in Chicago, and in Marquette Park, police power was employed to protect their rights. It cost $10,000 to clean up Marquette Park after the twenty-five Nazis demonstrated and $90,000 in overtime pay for the police. If the Nazis had gone ahead with their plan to march in Skokie, thousands of police would have been on hand to protect them at many times the cost of the Marquette Park rally.

The judges who devoted so much attention to the Nazis, the police departments that paid so much overtime, and the American Civil Liberties Union, which lost a half-million dollars in membership income as a consequence of its defense, used their time and money well. They defeated the Nazis by preserving the legitimacy of American democracy.

Index

ABOUT THE AUTHOR

For Aryeh Neier, defending the enemy has personal meaning. He was born in Berlin in 1937 of Jewish parents and at two years old escaped with his parents and sister to England from Nazi Germany. Most of the rest of his family was lost in the Holocaust. Now a visiting professor of law at New York University, Aryeh Neier served as national executive director of the American Civil Liberties Union from 1970 to 1978 and, before that, served as executive director of its New York affiliate for five years. He earlier was director of the League for Industrial Democracy. He is a contributing editor for *The Nation*, a fellow of the New York Institute for the Humanities, author of *Dossier: The Secret Files They Keep on You* and *Crime and Punishment: A Radical Solution*, and co-editor, with Norman Dorsen, of a series of books on peoples' rights.